GLORIOUS TRUTHS ABOUT
Emma Smith

OTHER BOOKS AND AUDIOBOOKS
BY SUSAN EASTON BLACK

400 Questions and Answers about the Book of Mormon

400 Questions and Answers about the Old Testament

*400 Questions and Answers about the
Life and Times of Jesus Christ*

400 Questions and Answers about the Doctrine and Covenants

Women of Character

Men of Character

Glorious Truths about Mother Eve

Glorious Truths about Mary, Mother of Jesus

GLORIOUS TRUTHS ABOUT
Emma Smith

SUSAN EASTON BLACK

Covenant Communications, Inc.

To Savi,
my beautiful and kind granddaughter

Cover image *All Things Dear* © Julie Rogers, for more information go to www.julierogersart.com

Cover design © 2020 by Covenant Communications, Inc.

Published by Covenant Communications, Inc.
American Fork, Utah

Copyright © 2020 by Susan Easton Black
All rights reserved. No part of this book may be reproduced in any format or in any medium without the written permission of the publisher, Covenant Communications, Inc., P.O. Box 416, American Fork, UT 84003. This work is not an official publication of The Church of Jesus Christ of Latter-day Saints. The views expressed within this work are the sole responsibility of the author and do not necessarily reflect the position of The Church of Jesus Christ of Latter-day Saints, Covenant Communications, Inc., or any other entity.

Printed in the United States of America
First Printing: March 2020

27 26 25 24 23 22 21 20   10 9 8 7 6 5 4 3 2 1

ISBN 978-1-52441-261-6

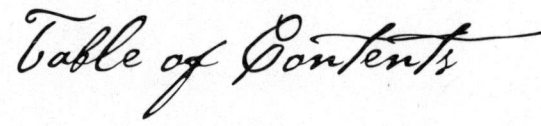
Table of Contents

Introduction..vii

Chapter One: Emma Hale Marries Joseph Smith..........................1

Chapter Two: The Book of Mormon and Emma............................7

Chapter Three: The Ohio Years...15

Chapter Four: The Tribulations of Missouri.................................25

Chapter Five: An Elect Lady..33

Chapter Six: The Martyrdom..43

Chapter Seven: Widow to Second Marriage.................................53

Chapter Eight: Choices..65

Chapter Nine: Conflict...75

Chapter Ten: The Last Years..83

Epilogue..91

Chronology of Emma Hale Smith Bidamon................................97

Introduction

GLORIOUS TRUTHS ABOUT EMMA SMITH is the third book in the series *Glorious Truths*. The first book was of Eve, the best-known woman in the Old Testament. Bible readers may have trouble recalling that Abraham married Sarai (Sarah) or that Dinah was the sister of Levi, but readers do not hesitate to answer the question "Who was the helpmeet of Adam?" However, some wonder whether Eve, the last of God's creations, was the perfect helpmeet. After all, she partook of the forbidden fruit and persuaded Adam to do likewise. When questions of Eve's actions in the Garden of Eden turn to discussion, Mother Eve enters a controversial arena of unfavorable proportions. Readers discovered in *Glorious Truths about Mother Eve* that neither the Lord nor His prophets have spoken disparagingly of her. Instead, they extoll the nobleness of Mother Eve, her role as matriarch of the human race, and her role as Adam's eternal companion.

The second book in the series was *Glorious Truths about Mary, Mother of Jesus*. Mary was the "virgin, most beautiful and fair" that Nephi saw in vision (1 Nephi 11:15). She was the mother of "The mighty God, The everlasting Father, The Prince of Peace" prophesied by Isaiah (Isaiah 9:6). Mary was the only woman mentioned by name before her birth in holy writ and the only mother who has known the joy of rearing a sinless son—a son whose life was a fulfillment of ancient prophecies that foretold his ministry, atonement, death, and resurrection.

The third in the series is *Glorious Truths about Emma Smith*. When Emma eloped with Joseph Smith and was married, she had no inkling that one day she would be the most famous woman in the history of The Church of Jesus Christ of Latter-day Saints. But as the years have passed, Emma, who wrote only a few letters and gave fewer speeches, is the one woman known among members of The Church of Jesus Christ of Latter-day Saints throughout the world.

It has been a joy to write about these three great women—Eve, Mary, and Emma. Their lives were filled with wonder, sacrifice, heartache, and eternal promises. To Emma, the last of the three, I express gratitude for standing by Joseph Smith in his extremities and for her sure testimony of the Book of Mormon and of Joseph's prophetic call.

Chapter One

EMMA HALE MARRIES JOSEPH SMITH

EMMA SMITH IS THE MOST famous woman in nineteenth-century Latter-day Saint history. Much has been spoken and written about her life—both positive and negative. The topic of her life has left more than one writer frustrated because Emma did not keep a journal, write an autobiography, or pen vignettes of key life events. Such omissions have left more than one biographer looking to the collected works of those who knew her best.

Those who knew of her suffering at the hands of outraged mobs and of her anguish at the deaths of infants seldom wrote of her heartaches. Although they were recipients of her generosity and kindness and witnessed her loyalty to her husband Joseph, she in no way dominated their writings. The extant letters exchanged between Joseph and Emma and letters between Emma's second husband, Lewis Bidamon, and herself and those of her children are filled with short snippets of life's experiences but leave the inquisitive wanting more.

In turning to primary sources, Joseph Smith's journal entries provide factual information but precious little commentary. For example, "Continued translating and revising, and reading letters in the evening Sister Emma being present in the office.";[1] "In the afternoon rode to Brother John Benbows on horseback accompanied by Emma and others";[2] "Rode to the big mound on the LaHarpe road accompanied—by Emma";[3] and "Spent the forenoon chiefly in conversation with Emma on various subjects, and in reading my history with her. Both felt in good spirits and very cheerful."[4] Letters from children and grandchildren give only glimpses into Emma's life, such as, "Every body

---

1   History, 1838–1856, volume C-1 [2 November 1838–31 July 1842], p. 1287 (9 March 1842). Joseph Smith Papers.
2   History, 1838–1856, volume C-1 [2 November 1838–31 July 1842], p. 1339 (3 June 1842). Joseph Smith Papers.
3   History, 1838–1856, volume C-1 [2 November 1838–31 July 1842], p. 1340 (14 June 1842). Joseph Smith Papers.
4   History, 1838–1856, volume D-1 [1 August 1842–1 July 1843], p. 1366 (14 August 1842). Joseph Smith Papers.

knew of Mother Bidamon's salves for cuts—bruises—fever—rheumatism—for every kind of ache & pain," leaving much to be surmised.[5] Friend and journalist Emmeline B. Wells penned, "[Emma] was a queen in her home, so to speak, and beloved by the people, who were many of them indebted to her for favors and kindnesses."[6] But the question of what favors and kindnesses begs for an answer.

Who was Emma Smith? Unable to dismiss the question, some biographers have placed Emma in settings not supported by historical evidence. They tell of feelings that may or may not have been hers when discussing sacred doctrines and her relationship with Joseph Smith. These writers use words like *perhaps* or *maybe* and phrases like *one can imagine* to interpret Emma's life. Their conclusions may not be correct and too often leave readers with more questions than answers. Then there are those who claim to have written about Emma, but in actuality, they clearly wrote the early history of the Restoration with only occasional mentions of her.

In an era when Latter-day Saints have a renewed interest in Emma Smith—her life, her thoughts, and her choices—a well-documented biographical approach is needed, regardless of its unavoidable brevity. Readers will discover in *Glorious Truths about Emma Smith* a brief, informative, and insightful approach to the life of Emma Smith. Facts presented in the text provide readers with a reason to consider and perhaps discard past judgmental assessments and erroneous conclusions. Facts may lead readers to embrace the charity of her life's work and emulate her charity in their own lives. Not every question about Emma is resolved in the text, but questions of her testimony of Joseph Smith's prophetic calling and the Book of Mormon are answered with clarity. Why read *Glorious Truths about Emma Smith*? From Emma's early days in Harmony to her last days in Nauvoo, Emma led an extraordinary life. Emma was the wife of the Prophet Joseph Smith, the first to know that Joseph received the plates from the angel Moroni, a scribe to the Book of Mormon translation, the mother of eleven children (raising five to adulthood), and president of the Female Relief Society of Nauvoo.

***

Emma Hale, the third daughter and seventh child of Isaac and Elizabeth Hale, was born on July 10, 1804, in Harmony, Pennsylvania. She grew to

---

5   Emma Smith McCallum's Reminiscences, as quoted in Buddy Youngreen, *Reflections of Emma, Joseph Smith's Wife* (Provo, UT: Maasai, Inc., 1982), 61.

6   Emmeline B. Wells, "L. D. S. Women of the Past. Personal Impressions," *Woman's Exponent* 36, no. 7 (February 1908): 490.

maturity in a comfortable home (foundation dimensions are thirty by forty-two feet) in Harmony's rural environs. In the home, she was taught early American culinary arts, like the use of herbal medicines and how to knit, sew, patch, and mend. Learning to dry fruit, make candles from tallow, and cure sausages was as important to her overall education as reading, writing, and arithmetic. Emma was religious by nature; she attended worship services with her parents and enjoyed singing hymns. Her father, Isaac, claimed to be "converted from deism to faith in Christ" by observing Emma pray in his behalf.[7]

Joseph Smith met Emma Hale when she was twenty-one years old. At that time, she stood five feet nine inches tall and had dark hair and hazel eyes. One historian described her as "well turned, of excellent form . . . with splendid physical development."[8] According to Lucy Mack Smith, Joseph "immediately commenced paying his addresses" to Emma.[9] Such attention was not pleasing to her father, Isaac Hale, who wrote,

> I first became acquainted with Joseph Smith, Jr. in November 1825. He was at that time in the employ of a set of men who were called "money-diggers," and his occupation was that of seeing, or pretending to see, by means of a stone placed in his hat, and his hat closed over his face. In this way he pretended to discover minerals and hidden treasure.[10]

Of his digging for treasures, Joseph wrote, "I continued to work for nearly a month without success in [my] undertaking, and finally I prevailed with the old gentleman to cease digging after it."[11] Digging stopped on November 17, 1825. Isaac Hale blamed Joseph for halting the digging. He wrote, "Young

---

7 Buddy Youngreen, *Reflections of Emma: Joseph Smith's Wife* (Orem, UT: Grandin Book Company, 1982), p. 5.

8 Inez A. Kennedy, *Recollections of the Pioneers of Lee County* (Dixon, IL: n.p. 1893), p. 96, as cited in Linda King Newell and Valeen Tipetts Avery, *Mormon Enigma: Emma Hale Smith* (Garden City, NY: Doubleday & Company, Inc., 1984). In January 1928 Samuel O. Bennion viewed Emma's skeletal remains and observed: "She must have been quite a large woman, because the bones in her legs were almost as long as the leg bones of the skeletons of Joseph and Hyrum." Samuel O. Bennion to Heber J. Grant and Counselors, January 21, 1928. Church History Library.

9 Lucy Mack Smith, History, 1845, p. 96. Joseph Smith Papers.

10 Statement of Isaac Hale, Affirmed to and subscribed before Chas. Dimon, J. P., March 20, 1834, as reprinted in Emily C. Blackman, *History of Susquehanna County, Pennsylvania*, p. 578, as cited in Susan Easton Black, "Isaac Hale: Antagonist of Joseph Smith," *Regional Studies in Latter-day Saint Church History: New York*. Larry C. Porter, Milton V. Backman Jr., and Susan Easton Black ed. (Provo, UT: BYU Department of Church History and Doctrine, 1992), p. 98.

11 History, 1838–1856, vol. A-1 of *The Joseph Smith Papers* [23 December 1805–30 August 1834], 8.

Smith gave the money-diggers great encouragement at first, but, when they had arrived in digging to [sic] near the place where he had stated an immense treasure would be found, he said the enchantment was so powerful that he could not see it."[12] His allegation lacks support from other witnesses of the treasure digging and may have its roots in later animosity between Isaac Hale and Joseph.

Isaac Hale's animosity grew in intensity when the digging stopped. Due to his angry feelings, Joseph left the Hale home and boarded with Josiah Stowell near South Bainbridge. Stowell employed him as a farmhand cutting timber. When not working for Stowell, Joseph was courting Emma. Isaac wrote, "Young Smith made several visits at my house, and at length asked my consent to his marrying my daughter Emma. This I refused, and gave him my reasons for so doing; some of which were, that he was a stranger, and followed a business that I could not approve."[13]

Joseph's frequent visits to see Emma were interrupted in March 1826, when he was arrested and brought to trial in South Bainbridge. Peter Bridgeman, a nephew of Mrs. Stowell, claimed Joseph was a disorderly person and an imposter. Diverse accounts of the trial exist, but all accounts agree that Joseph's seer stone was widely discussed.[14]

Following the trial, Joseph's attentions once again turned to Emma. To his dismay, Emma's brothers, who had been reasonably accommodating toward him, were now in league with their father. Undeterred, Joseph asked Joseph Knight to furnish him a horse and sled so that he could go see Emma. When the Hale family rebuffed him again, Joseph left the area and returned to the Smith farmhouse in New York.

Joseph confided in his mother that "no young woman that he ever [saw] was acquainted with was better calculated to render the man of her choice happy than Miss Emma Hale a young lady of whom he had been extremely fond of since his first introduction to her."[15] According to Mother Smith, Joseph said, "I have been very lonely ever since Alvin—[his brother] died, and I have concluded to get married; and, if you have no objections, Miss Emma Hale would be my

---

12 Statement of Isaac Hale in Blackman, *History of Susquehanna County, Pennsylvania*, 578, cited in Black, "Isaac Hale: Antagonist of Joseph Smith," p. 99.
13 Ibid., p. 100.
14 Oliver Cowdery reported that "some verry officious persons complained of [Joseph] as a disorderly person, and brought him before the authorities of the county; but there being no cause of action he was honorably acquitted." Oliver Cowdery to W. W. Phelps, "Letter No. II," *Messenger and Advocate* 2, no. 1 (October 1835) 201.
15 Lucy Mack Smith, History, 1844–1845, p. [10], bk. 4. Joseph Smith Papers.

choice before any other woman I have ever seen."[16] Knowing Joseph's feelings about Emma, Mother Smith wrote, "[We were] highly pleased with the choice which Joseph made in a wife and told him [we were] not only willing that he should marry her but desired him to bring her home with him that we might have the pleasure of her society."[17]

Joseph journeyed to Pennsylvania in the winter of 1827 with plans to marry Emma and bring her back to New York. He wrote, "[Isaac] was greatly opposed to our being married, in so much that he would not suffer us to be married at his house, I was therefore under the necessity of taking her elsewhere."[18] On January 18, 1827, Joseph and Emma were wed in South Bainbridge, New York. Of her marriage, Emma said to her son Joseph Smith III,

> I was married at South Bainbridge, New York. . . . at the house of Squire Tarbell, by him . . . I had no intention of marrying when I left home; but, during my visit at Mr. Stowell's, your father visited me there. My folks were bitterly opposed to him; and, being importuned by your father, aided by Mr. Stowell, who urged me to marry, and preferring to marry him to any other man I knew, I consented. . . . when father found that I was married, he sent for us.[19]

Isaac's reaction to the marriage of Joseph and Emma was one of distress. He claimed that his twenty-two-year-old daughter had been abducted by a "careless young man, not very well educated." He wrote, "While I was absent from home, [Joseph] carried off my daughter into the State of New York, where they were married."[20] Mother Smith's reaction to their elopement was quite the opposite:

> I set myself to work to put my house in order, for the reception of my son's bride; and I felt all that pride and ambition in doing so, that is common to mothers upon such occasions. My

---

16 Lucy Mack Smith, History, 1845, p. 97. Joseph Smith Papers.
17 Lucy Mack Smith, History, 1844–1845, Document Transcript, bk. 4. Joseph Smith Papers.
18 History, circa June 1839–circa 1841 [Draft 2], p. 8. Joseph Smith Papers.
19 Joseph Smith III, "Last Testimony of Sister Emma," *The Saints' Herald* 26, no. 19 (October 1, 1879): 101 & 289.
20 Statement of Isaac Hale in Blackman, *History of Susquehanna County, Pennsylvania*, 578, as cited in Susan Easton Black, "Isaac Hale: Antagonist of Joseph Smith," *Regional Studies in Latter-day Saint Church History: New York* (Provo, UT: Department of Church History and Doctrine, Brigham Young University, 1992), p. 101.

oldest son had, previous to this, formed a matrimonial relation with one of the most excellent of women; with whom I had seen much enjoyment; and I hoped for as much happiness with my second [daughter-in-law], as I had received from the society of the first, and there was no reason why I should expect anything to the contrary.[21]

Believing a warm welcome awaited them in Palmyra, Joseph wrote, "Immediately after my marriage I . . . went to my father's and farmed with him that season."[22] From the Smith farmhouse, Emma corresponded with her father, asking him if she could have her clothing, furniture, cow, and other articles. Despite his earlier anger over her marriage to Joseph, Isaac responded kindlier than might have been expected: "Her property was safe and at her disposal."[23]

In August 1827, eight months after their marriage, Joseph and Emma returned to Harmony to face Isaac. Isaac said to Joseph, "You have stolen my daughter and married her. I had much rather have followed her to her grave. You spend your time digging for money—pretend to see in a stone, and thus try to deceive people."[24] Yet in this visit, there was a reconciliation between Joseph and his father-in-law. An invitation was extended for Joseph and Emma to make their home in Harmony if Joseph would give up "his old practice of looking in the stone." Isaac promised to assist Joseph in getting into a business, and "Smith stated to me he had given up what he called 'glass-looking,' and that he expected and was willing to work hard for a living," Isaac reported.[25] In the meanwhile, Joseph and Emma returned to the home of Joseph Smith Sr. in western New York.

---

21 Lucy Mack Smith, History, 1845, p. 97. Joseph Smith Papers.
22 Smith, *History of the Church*, 1:17; History, circa June 1839–circa 1841 [Draft 2], p. 17. Joseph Smith Papers.
23 Statement of Isaac Hale in Blackman, *History of Susquehanna County, Pennsylvania*, 578, cited in Black, "Isaac Hale: Antagonist of Joseph Smith," p. 101.
24 Statement of Isaac Hale, in Howe, *Mormonism Unvailed* (Painesville, OH: E. B. Howe, 1834), p. 330.
25 Statement of Isaac Hale in Blackman, *History of Susquehanna County, Pennsylvania*, 578, cited in Black, "Isaac Hale: Antagonist of Joseph Smith," p. 102.

Chapter Two

THE BOOK OF MORMON AND EMMA

On September 20, 1827, "Mr. Knight [Joseph Knight Sr.] and his friend Stoal [Josiah Stowell] came to see how we were managing matters . . . and staid with us," wrote Mother Smith.[1] It is presumed that Knight and Stowell knew the significance of September 21, for Knight reported that Joseph "made known [to] us that he had seen a vision, that a personage had appeared to him, and told him where there was a gold book of ancient date buried, and that if he would follow the direction of the angel, he could get it. We were told this in secret."[2] On that night, Lucy Mack Smith sat "up very late, as my work rather pressed upon my hands."

About midnight, Joseph asked if she possessed "a chest with a lock and key." Mother Smith penned, "I knew in an instant what he wanted it for; and not having one I was greatly alarmed; as I thought it might be a matter of considerable moment. But Joseph, discovering my anxiety, said: 'never mind, I can do very well for the present without it—be calm, all is right.'"[3] A short while later, Emma passed through the room where Lucy was sitting. She was wearing "her bonnet and riding dress." Together Joseph and Emma left the farmhouse, took "Mr. Knight's horse and wagon," and drove to the hill.[4] Emma waited in the wagon while Joseph climbed the hill and there conversed with the angel Moroni. Joseph wrote,

---

1 Lucy Mack Smith, History, 1845, p. 105 (20 September 1827). Joseph Smith Papers.
2 Joseph Knight, Jr., "Incidents of History," as cited in William G. Hartley, "Close Friends as Witnesses: Joseph Smith and the Joseph Knight Families," in Susan Easton Black and Charles D. Tate Jr., *Joseph Smith: The Prophet, The Man* (Provo, UT: Religious Studies Center Brigham Young University, 1993), p. 272.
3 Lucy Mack Smith, History, 1845, p. 105 (20 September 1827). Joseph Smith Papers.
4 Lucy Mack Smith, History, 1845, ch. 23, p. 105. Joseph Smith Papers. Joseph Knight penned, "the 'personage' [a reference to angel Moroni] told him he could have the record the following September 'if he brought with him the right person' and indicated that Joseph would know who that was." Joseph Knight, in whom Joseph later confided the story, said the young man "looked into his glass and found it was Emma Hale Daughter of old Mr. Hale of Pensulvany." See Hartley, "Close Friends as Witnesses: Joseph Smith and the Joseph Knight Families," in *Joseph Smith: The Prophet, The Man*, p. 272.

> The same heavenly messenger delivered [the plates] up to me with this charge: that I should be responsible for them; that if I should let them go carelessly, or through any neglect of mine, I should be cut off; but that if I would use all my endeavors to preserve them, until he, the messenger, should call for them, they should be protected. (JS–H 1:59)

When Joseph returned to the wagon with plates in hand, Emma was the first to know that he had received the gold plates from the angel Moroni.

When Joseph and Emma returned to the farmhouse "nothing [was] said about where they had been," wrote Joseph Knight:

> After breakfast Joseph called me into the other room . . . He set his foot on the bed and leaned his head on his hand and said . . . "It is ten times better than I expected." Then he went on to tell length and width and thickness of the plates, and said he, "They appear to be gold." But he seemed to think more of the glasses or the urim and thummim than he did of the plates, for, said he, "I can see anything; they are marvelous. Now they are written in characters and I want them translated."[5]

Joseph Knight and others in the Smith household rejoiced that day. Joseph cautioned them to keep their joy a secret, for "satan had stirred up the hearts of those who had barely a hint of the Matter to search into it and make every possible move towards preventing the work."[6] Although they promised to keep news of the unearthed treasure a secret, rumors of gold plates flew through the village of Palmyra as if on the wings of eagles.

As word of gold treasure spread from house to house, assailants tried to take what they called "Joe Smith's Gold Bible." Cash and property were offered to Joseph for a glimpse of the plates. When he refused, schemes were contrived to snatch the treasure. A mob element shouted, "We will have the plates in spite of Joe Smith or all the Devils in Hell."[7]

Keeping the plates safe and out of sight proved difficult for Joseph. A birch log, hearthstones, floorboards, flax, and a barrel of beans were used to hide the plates and keep thieves at bay. But there was little stopping mobocracy

---

5   Dean C. Jessee, "Joseph Knight's Recollection of Early Mormon History," *BYU Studies* 17, no. 1 (Autumn 1976): 33. Spelling standardized; Reminiscences of Joseph Knight, in "Moroni: Messenger of the Restoration." churchofjesuschrist.org.
6   Lucy Mack Smith, History, 1844–1845, Document Transcript, Book 5. Joseph Smith Papers.
7   Lucy Mack Smith, History, 1844–1845, p. 9, Book 5. Joseph Smith Papers.

from mushrooming. Instead of being frustrated in their attempts to find the treasure, would-be thieves grew more vigilant. As frenzy over the "Gold Bible" mounted, Joseph was "under the necessity of leaving" the area.[8] As difficult as his relationship had been with his father-in-law, Isaac Hale, he was the only choice.

Alvah Hale, son of Isaac Hale, was sent by his father to convey Joseph and Emma and their personal property (which included a chest that contained the plates, the breastplate, and the Urim and Thummim hidden in a barrel) to Harmony. The threesome arrived in the village of Harmony in December 1827. Joseph and Emma moved into a small three-room house (twenty-four by fourteen feet) located about 150 yards from the Isaac Hale farmhouse. Joseph purchased the small house and thirteen and a half acres of farmland from his father-in-law for two hundred dollars. Immediate payment was not expected.

In the confines of their small home, the plates "lay in a box under our bed for months," Emma recalled. "But I never felt at liberty to look at them."[9] She added, "[They] often lay on the table without any attempt at concealment, wrapped in a small linen table cloth, which I had given him to fold them in. I once felt of the plates, as they thus lay on the table, tracing their outline and shape." To Emma, the plates "seemed to be pliable like thick paper, and would rustle with a metallic sound when the edges were moved by the thumb, as one does sometimes thumb the edges of a book."[10]

Joseph and Emma had several visitors in their home that winter. None stayed longer than Martin Harris, who scribed the Book of Lehi as Joseph translated from the gold plates. Father and Mother Smith also visited and took occasion to become "acquainted with Emma's father . . . [and] family." Mother Smith wrote, "They were an intelligent and highly respectable family."[11] Another guest was Lucy Harris, the wife of Martin Harris. "Without delay she commenced ransacking every nook and corner about the house—chests, trunks, cupboards, etc." looking for the gold plates.[12] Not finding them in the house, she searched out-of-doors. Returning to the house "rather ill-natured," she asked Emma "if there were snakes in that country in the winter."[13] Emma assured Lucy that there were no snakes out in the winter months. Lucy Harris retorted, "I have

---

8 History, 1838–1856, volume A-1 [23 December 1805–30 August 1834], Document Transcript, September 1827–February 1828. Joseph Smith Papers.
9 Emma Smith quoted in Newell and Avery, *Mormon Enigma*, p. 298.
10 Smith, "Last Testimony of Sister Emma," *Saints' Herald* 26, no. 19 (October 1, 1879): 290.
11 Lucy Mack Smith, History, 1845, p. 139. Joseph Smith Papers.
12 Lucy Mack Smith, History, 1845. Document transcript, ch. 24, 123–124. Joseph Smith Papers.
13 Lucy Mack Smith, History.

been walking about in the woods to look at the situation of your place, and, as I turned round to come home a tremendous black snake stuck up his head before me and commenced hissing at me." Lucy explained that this "gave her a terrible fright," and she "ran with all possible speed to the house."[14] The tale ended as quickly as Lucy's search for the gold plates. Lucy left the Smith farmhouse. Her remaining days in Harmony, she lived with a neighbor and spoke disparagingly of Joseph as a grand impostor to anyone who would listen. Visibly upset by her words and actions, a disgruntled Martin Harris took his wife, Lucy, back to Palmyra.

The Tragic Events of 1828

As winter turned to spring, difficulties marred the lives of Joseph and Emma. Martin Harris took the 116-page manuscript with him to Palmyra to show his wife and family members. The day after Martin left, on June 15, 1828, Emma gave birth to a son, Alvin. Alvin died within hours of his birth and was buried east of their home. Midwife Rhoda Skinner claimed the child had birth defects. Sophia Lewis, who claimed to be "present at the birth of this child," spoke of the child being "still-born and very much deformed."[15]

As for Emma, she "seemed to tremble upon the verge of the silent home of her infant, so uncertain seemed her fate for a season that in the space of 2 weeks [Joseph] never slept one hour in undisturbed quiet."[16] As Emma began to recover, her thoughts turned to Martin Harris. He had not returned to Harmony as promised; it had been nearly three weeks (June 14, 1828, to July 7, 1828) since he left Harmony with the manuscript pages. "I cannot rest and shall not be at ease untill [sic] I know something about what Mr. Harris is doing," Emma said.[17] She insisted that Joseph journey to Palmyra and learn why Martin had delayed his return.

At first Joseph protested, but "seeing her so cheerful, and so willing to have him leave,"[18] he consented. Soon after he reached the Smith farmhouse, Joseph learned from Martin Harris that the Book of Lehi manuscript was missing and possibly lost. Difficult days followed. Joseph supplicated the Lord without ceasing for forgiveness of his sins. It was not until September 22, 1828, that Joseph "had the joy and satisfaction of again receiving the Urim and Thummim."[19]

---

14 Lucy Mack Smith, History, 1845, p. 125. Joseph Smith Papers.
15 *Amboy Journal*, August 6, 1879 as cited in Newell and Avery, *Mormon Enigma*, p. 27.
16 Lucy Mack Smith, History, 1844–1845, pgs. [1-2], bk. 7. Joseph Smith Papers.
17 Lucy Mack Smith, History, 1844–1845, p. [2], bk. 7. Spelling standardized. Joseph Smith Papers.
18 Lucy Mack Smith, History, 1845. Document transcript, ch. 25, 127. Joseph Smith Papers.
19 Lucy Mack Smith, History, 1845, p. 138. Joseph Smith Papers.

The Book of Mormon

Emma was asked to serve as Joseph's scribe as he translated the Book of Mormon. "If I made any mistake in spelling," she said, "he would stop me and correct my spelling, although it was impossible for him to see how I was writing them down at the time. Even the word 'Sar[i]ah' he could not pronounce at first, but had to spell it, and I would pronounce it for him." At one point he asked, "'Emma, did Jerusalem have walls surrounding it?' When I informed him that it had, Joseph replied, 'Oh! I was afraid I had been deceived.'"[20]

Emma was questioned about her role in the coming forth of the Book of Mormon by her son Joseph Smith III:

> Q. I should suppose that you would have uncovered the plates and examined them?
> A. I did not attempt to handle the plates, other than I have told you, nor uncover them to look at them. I was satisfied that it was the work of God, and therefore did not feel it to be necessary to do so . . . I moved them from place to place on the table, as it was necessary in doing my work.
> Q. Had he not a book or manuscript from which he read, or dictated to you?
> A. He had neither manuscript nor book to read from.
> Q. Could he not have had, and you not [k]now it?
> A. If he had anything of the kind he could not have concealed it from me.
> Q. Could not father have dictated the Book of Mormon to you, Oliver Cowdery and the others who wrote for him, after having first written it, or having first read it out of some book?
> A. Joseph Smith could neither write nor dictate a coherent and well-worded letter; let alone dictating a book like the Book of Mormon. And, though I was an active participant in the scenes that transpired, and was present during the translation of the plates, and had cognizance of things as they transpired, it is marvelous to me, "a marvel and a wonder," as much as to anyone else.
> Q. Mother, what is your belief about the authenticity, or origin of the Book of Mormon?
> A. My belief is that the Book of Mormon is of divine authenticity—I have not the slightest doubt of it. I am

---

20 Edmund C. Briggs, "A Visit to Nauvoo in 1856," *Journal of History* 9 (October 1916): 454.

satisfied that no man could have dictated the writing of the manuscripts unless he was inspired; for, when acting as his scribe, your father would dictate to me hour after hour; and when returning after meals, or after interruptions, he would at once begin where he had left off, without either seeing the manuscript or having any portion of it read to him. This was a usual thing for him to do. It would have been improbable that a learned man could do this; and, for one so ignorant and unlearned as he was, it was simply impossible.[21]

Emma's brief but unfailing testimony of the coming forth of the Book of Mormon uttered near the end of her life has given generations of believers a reason to pause and reflect upon the truth of her words.

As the work of translation moved forward, Oliver Cowdery replaced Emma as the scribe for the Book of Mormon translation. Oliver later testified, "I wrote with my own pen the entire Book of Mormon (save a few pages) as it fell from the lips of the Prophet, as he translated it by the gift and power of God, by means of the Urim and Thummim. . . . That book is true."[22]

***

The translation moved forward in spite of verbal threats against Joseph and Oliver. To the credit of Isaac Hale, he spoke out against violence and quelled the threat of mobocracy in Harmony. Such could not be said of Nathaniel Lewis, the Methodist preacher in the village and uncle of Emma. Nathaniel was indignant when he learned that Isaac and his family had promised Joseph and Oliver protection. He told Isaac "falsehoods concerning [Joseph] of the most shameful nature, which turned the old gentleman and his family so much against [Joseph and Oliver], that they would no longer promise . . . protection."[23]

Without Isaac's protection and with menacing threats from local citizens "to prevent the work of God from going forth to the world," Joseph and Oliver fled from Harmony to the home of Peter Whitmer Sr. in Fayette, New York.[24] Emma soon joined them.

---

21   Joseph Smith III, "Last Testimony of Sister Emma," *The Saints' Herald* 26, no. 19 (October 1, 1879): 289.
22   Reuben Miller, October 21, 1848, Church History Library. See also Richard L. Anderson, "By the Gift and Power of God," *Ensign*, September 1977.
23   Blackman, *History of Susquehanna County, Pennsylvania*, p. 579, cited in Black, "Isaac Hale: Antagonist of Joseph Smith," p. 104.
24   Lucy Mack Smith, History, 1845, p. 149. Joseph Smith Papers.

Joseph "worked from morning till night" in the Whitmer log home to complete the Book of Mormon translation.[25] As Joseph's work neared completion, David Whitmer witnessed an unpleasant exchange between Joseph and Emma:

> Something went wrong about the house and he was put out about it. Something that Emma, his wife, had done. Oliver and I went upstairs, and Joseph came up soon after to continue the translation, but he could not do anything. He could not translate a single syllable. He went downstairs, out into the orchard, and made supplication to the Lord; was gone about an hour—came back to the house, and asked Emma's forgiveness and then came upstairs where we were and the translation went on all right.[26]

As the translation neared completion, Joseph made preparations for publishing the Book of Mormon. After obtaining a copyright on June 11, 1829, from R. R. Lansing, he secured the printing services of Egbert B. Grandin of Palmyra. Publishing five thousand copies of the Book of Mormon took time. It was not until March 26, 1830 that Grandin announced the Book of Mormon was published and for sale at his bookstore.

It was her testimony of the Book of Mormon, the prophetic calling of her husband, and the organization of a Church on April 6, 1830, that led Emma to enter baptismal waters on June 28, 1830. She was baptized by Oliver Cowdery. When asked years later about the reasons behind her decision to be baptized, Emma said, "I know Mormonism to be the truth; and believe the Church to have been established by divine direction. I have complete faith in it."[27]

Days after Emma's baptism, in early July 1830, Joseph Smith received a revelation affirming her "sins are forgiven" and she was "an elect lady" (D&C 25:3). Emma was told in the revelation to "murmur not because of the things which thou hast not seen, for they are withheld from thee and from the world," an apparent reference to the gold plates (D&C 25:4). Her "office" was to be "a comfort unto my servant, Joseph Smith, Jun., thy husband" and speak "consoling words, in the spirit of meekness" to him (D&C 25:5). She was to

---

25 *Deseret Evening News*, March 25, 1884, as cited in Richard L. Bushman, *Joseph Smith and the Beginnings of Mormonism* (Urbana and Chicago: University of Illinois Press, 1984), pp. 103–104.
26 William H. Kelley and G. A. Blakeslee, "Letter from Elder W. H. Kelley, 15 January 1882, Richmond, Missouri," *Saints' Herald* 29, no. 5 (March 1, 1882): 68.
27 Smith, "Last Testimony of Sister Emma," *Saints' Herald* 26, no. 19 (October 1, 1879): 290.

"go with him at the time of his going, and be unto him for a scribe" (D&C 25:6). For faithfully fulfilling these divine directives, Emma was promised that her "husband shall support thee in the church" (D&C 25:9). The revelation ended with a phrase of hope: "Lift up thy heart and rejoice, and cleave unto the covenants which thou has made . . . a crown of righteousness thou shalt receive" (D&C 25:13, 15).

Chapter Three
THE OHIO YEARS

In December 1830, Joseph Smith received a revelation commanding him and his followers to leave western New York "because of the enemy and for your sake" (D&C 37:1). In compliance with the revelation, Emma prepared to leave New York. In the winter of 1831, she travelled with Joseph in a crowded sleigh from New York to Ohio. On February 1, 1831, they arrived in Kirtland, Ohio.

Joseph alighted from the sleigh, walked up the steps of the Gilbert and Whitney store, and exclaimed to the man standing on the porch, "Newel K. Whitney! Thou art the man!" Whitney replied, "You have the advantage of me . . . I could not call you by name as you have me." Joseph said, "I am Joseph, the Prophet . . . You've prayed me here, now what do you want of me?"[1] Newel Whitney, like most converts in Ohio, wanted to hear gospel truths from the Lord's Prophet. However, before any preaching could take place, Joseph and Emma were in need of lodging, especially Emma, for she was pregnant with twins. Algernon Sidney Gilbert, Whitney's partner, extended an invitation to the Smiths to reside in his home. When Emma saw the crowded living conditions in the Gilbert home, she refused his offer.

Joseph and Emma resided with the Whitneys for a time. Newel and his wife, Elizabeth, were pleased to host the Smiths, but Elizabeth's sister, "Aunt Sarah," was quite contrary about the matter. Within a month, Joseph and Emma had moved to a single-room cabin on the Isaac Morley farm a few miles north of Kirtland. Emma took up housekeeping, although there were few provisions and precious little furniture in the cabin.

On April 30, 1831, Emma gave birth to twins. Unfortunately, the twins—a boy and a girl—lived only a few hours. The next day, on May 1, 1831, Julia Clapp Murdock died giving birth to twins, a boy and a girl. "Bro. [John]

---

1   "Newel K. Whitney Store." churchofjesuschrist.org.

Murdock came to me and asked me to take them, and I took the babes [Joseph and Julia]," Emma wrote.²

Hiram, Ohio

In September 1831, Joseph, Emma, and the twins moved into the John Johnson farmhouse in Hiram, Ohio, about thirty miles from Kirtland. There they enjoyed a period of peace until March 1832, when the twins contracted measles. On the evening of March 24, 1832, a dozen men broke into the bedroom that Joseph, Emma, and the twins occupied in the farmhouse. The men grabbed at Joseph's "shirt, drawers and limbs." His struggle to free himself spawned threats of death. "[This] quieted me," Joseph wrote. "You will have mercy and spare my life, I hope." The profane response was "Call on yer God for help, we'll show ye no mercy." Joseph reported, the men intended to "beat and scratch me well, tear off my shirt and drawers, and leave me naked."³ They then tarred and feathered him—feathers symbolizing that the mob mocked Joseph and his teachings. Confident their dark deed had left him dead, the lawless intruders scattered into the shadows of the night.

Although Joseph survived the ordeal, his eleven-month-old son, Joseph Murdock Smith, did not. This was not the death the angry mob had planned that cold night in March. They had wanted nothing less than the death of Joseph, "the Mormon Prophet," not his young son. Yet the mob had caused doors to gape wide open, exposing the child to the frigid winter weather.

Knowing the animosity of the mob element in Hiram, Joseph fled from the rural community to Independence, Missouri, traveling nearly eight hundred miles. As he traveled toward Missouri, he was threatened by men, who pursued him from Hiram to Cincinnati. Seeing that the mob was not appeased, he now feared for the immediate safety of Emma and Julia. He wrote to Emma advising her to quickly move back to Kirtland and stay with Newel K. Whitney's family. "God is my friend in him I shall find comfort," he wrote to Emma. "I have given my life into his hands . . . I Count not my life dear to me only to do his will."⁴ On April 24, 1832, he arrived in Independence exactly one month to the day of his being tarred and feathered.

Unfortunately, Joseph found in Independence the same prejudice and hatred he had fled from in Hiram. The Latter-day Saints had settled "among a ferocious set of mobbers, like lambs among wolves."⁵ Joseph counseled them to

---

2   Smith, "Last Testimony of Sister Emma," *Saints' Herald* 26, no. 19 (October 1, 1879): 290.
3   Smith, *History of the Church*, 1:261, 1:263.
4   Letter of Joseph Smith to Emma Smith, June 6, 1832, p. [2]. Joseph Smith Papers.
5   History, 1838–1856, volume A-1 [23 December 1805–30 August 1834], p. 213. Joseph Smith Papers.

rise above retaliation and resolve to build homes in spite of outward challenges. Encouraged by his words and with resolute determination, the Saints clutched hammers, shovels, and spades and began anew to build what they hoped would be permanency.

In Joseph's Absence

As for Emma, her sorrow ran as deep as her fears in Joseph's absence. She no longer felt safe in the Johnson farmhouse in Hiram. With Joseph in Missouri, Emma returned with her baby, Julia, to Kirtland. She spent the late spring and early summer of 1832 shuffling between the homes of Reynolds Cahoon and Dr. F. G. Williams, occasionally spending time with Father and Mother Smith. "[Emma] labored faithfully for the interest of those with whom She staid, cheering them by her lively and spirited conversation," Mother Smith wrote.[6] "Her whole heart was in the work of the Lord and she felt no interest except for the church and the cause of truth whatever Her hands found to do she did with her might and did not ask the selfish question shall I be benefited any more than anyone else?"[7]

Not knowing of Emma's circumstance, Joseph chided her in a letter on June 6, 1832. "Being unwell [myself] at that time and filled with much anxiety it would have been very consoling to me to have received a few lines from you but as you did not take the trouble I will try to be contented with my lot knowing that God is my friend in him I shall find comfort."[8] When Joseph returned to Kirtland and grasped Emma's situation, he procured a home for his family—three storage rooms above the Gilbert and Whitney store. After making his family as comfortable as possible under these circumstances, Joseph left Kirtland to serve a short mission in the East. He wrote to Emma on October 13, 1832, from New York City:

> This day I have been walking through the most splendid part of the City of New Y[ork] – the buildings are truly great and wonderful . . . I returned to my room to meditate and calm my mind and behold the thoughts of home of Emma and Julia [M. Smith] rushes upon my mind like a flood and I could wish for [a] moment to be with them my breast is filled with all the feelings and tenderness of a parent and a Husband . . . I feel as if I wanted to say something to you to comfort you in your

---

6   Lucy Mack Smith, History, 1844–1845, p. [[8], bk. 13]. Joseph Smith Papers.
7   Lucy Mack Smith, History, 1844–1845, Document Transcript, bk. 13. Joseph Smith Papers.
8   Letter of Joseph Smith to Emma Smith, 6 June 1832, p. [2]. Joseph Smith Papers.

[peculiar] trial and present affliction I hope God will give you strength that you may not faint I pray God to soften the hearts of those arou[n]d you to be kind to you . . . you must cumfort [sic] yourself knowing that God is your friend in heaven and that you have one true and living friend on Earth your Husband.[9]

The "peculiar trial and present affliction" that Joseph wrote of was her pregnancy. Three weeks after receiving his letter, on November 6, 1832, Emma gave birth to Joseph Smith III in an upstairs room over the Gilbert and Whitney store. There were now two children in the Smith household—Julia and Joseph III. The burden of their care rested upon Emma.

Construction of the Kirtland Temple

For Joseph, there was a house to build—"a house, even a house of prayer, a house of fasting, a house of faith, a house of learning, a house of glory, a house of order, a house of God" (D&C 88:119). Work on the Kirtland Temple commenced. By late summer, nearly every able-bodied Saint had contributed time and labor to its construction. From cutting stones to felling trees, the men worked at a hurried pace to build the temple walls. Emma joined with the sisters in creating beautiful adornments for the interior of the temple. "Our wives were all the time knitting, spinning and sewing, and, in fact, I may say doing all kinds of work," Heber C. Kimball said. "They were just as busy as any of us."[10]

A few men waited until the afternoon hours to labor on the temple. In the morning hours, they attended the School of the Prophets that met above the Gilbert and Whitney store. Brigham Young recalled,

> When they assembled together in this room after breakfast, the first thing they did was to light their pipes, and, while smoking, talk about the great things of the kingdom, and spit all over the room, and as soon as the pipe was out [of] their mouths a large chew of tobacco would then be taken. Often when the Prophet entered the room to give the school instructions he would find himself in a cloud of tobacco smoke.[11]

---

9 Letter of Joseph Smith to Emma Smith, 13 October 1832, p. [2]. Spelling standardized. Joseph Smith Papers.
10 Heber C. Kimball, "Building the Temple.—Endowments.—Counsel to Missionaries, etc.," *Journal of Discourses*, 10:165.
11 Brigham Young, "School of the Prophets—Improvement of Provo City—Mitigation—Injudicious Trading," *Journal of Discourses*, 12:158.

Emma was not pleased. According to David Whitmer, she remarked to Joseph, "It would be a good thing if a revelation could be had declaring the use of tobacco a sin, and commanding its suppression." Whitmer recalled, "The matter was taken up and joked about, one of the brethren suggested that the revelation should also provide for a total abstinence from tea and coffee drinking, intending this as a counter dig at the sisters."[12] For Joseph, the issue was not a laughing matter but a matter of prayer. On February 27, 1833, he received the Word of Wisdom from the Lord and learned that "tobacco is not for the body, neither for the belly" (D&C 89:8).

By winter of 1833–1834, neighbors had threatened destruction of the temple walls and of the Prophet Joseph. "We had to guard night after night," Heber C. Kimball penned. "[We] were obliged to lie with our fire-locks in our arms, to preserve Brother Joseph's life."[13] For weeks, men did not remove their work clothes and "gave no sleep to their eyes, nor slumber to their eyelids," wanting to protect the temple walls and the life of the Prophet Joseph.[14] Notwithstanding threats, temple construction went steadily forward.

Zion's Camp

Mob violence was not kept at bay in the frontier settlement of Independence, Missouri. "All my property was scattered to the four winds, tools and all for pretended claims, where I owed not one cent justly," wrote Levi Hancock, a convert in Kirtland who was residing in Independence.[15] "We were threatened day and night. They told us they would burn our house down over our heads," wrote Isaac Morley. "The mob gave us no peace and all the while telling us we had to leave the country or they would kills us."[16] In November 1833, Latter-day Saints in Independence fled from unrestrained mobs across the Missouri River. Without adequate shelter and food, many of them suffered from illness. "The situation of the saints, as scattered, is dubious, and affords a gloomy prospect," W. W. Phelps wrote.[17]

When Joseph received word of the distressing circumstances of the Missouri Saints, he was "overwhelmed with grief. He burst into tears and sobbed aloud,

---

12 Des Moines *Daily News*, October 16, 1886, p. 20, as cited in Newell and Avery, *Mormon Enigma*, p. 47.
13 Orson F. Whitney, *Life of Heber C. Kimball, an Apostle, the Father and Founder of the British Mission* (Salt Lake City: Juvenile Instructor Office, 1888), p. 46.
14 Lucy Mack Smith, History, 1845, Document Transcript, ch. 44. Joseph Smith Papers.
15 Autobiography of Levi Ward Hancock, typescript, p. 50. L. Tom Perry Special Collections, Harold B. Lee Library, Brigham Young University, Provo, UT.
16 John Clifton Moffitt, "Isaac Morley on the American Frontier," n.p., n.d. In author's possession.
17 History, 1838–1856, volume A-1 [23 December 1805–30 August 1834], p. 397 (15 December 1833). Joseph Smith Papers.

'Oh, my brethren! my brethren' . . . would that I had been with you to have shared your fate. Oh my God, what shall I do in such a trial as this."[18] Wanting to relieve the suffering of the Missouri Saints and return them to their properties in Independence, Joseph formed a quasi-military force—Zion's Camp.

As the camp marched from Ohio to Missouri, Joseph counseled the men to keep the commandments of God, promising them deliverance from their enemies for obedience. In May 1834, Joseph wrote to Emma:

> I sit down in my tent to write a few lines to you to let you know that you are on my mind and that I am sensible of the dut[i]es of a Husband and Father and that I am well and I pray God to let his blessings rest upon you and the Children and all that are a round you until I return to your society . . . O may the blessings of God rest upon you is the prayre [sic] of your Husband until death.[19]

The next time Joseph wrote to Emma was on June 4, 1834, while encamped on the banks of the Mississippi River—

> Continue to pray to the Lord to hasten the day when we shall be permitted to behold each other's face again and enjoy the blessing of the family circle in peace and in righteousness . . . I have been able to endure the fatigue of the journey far beyond my most sanguine expectations, except have been troubled some with lameness, have had my feet blistered, but are now well, . . . were it not that every now and then our thoughts linger with inexpressible anxiety for our wives and our children our kindred according to the flesh who are entwined around our hearts; And also our brethren and friends; our whole journey would be as a dream, and this would be the happiest period of all our lives.[20]

Yet as days extended into weeks, problems surfaced. No problem caused more fear than the outbreak of infectious cholera that spread from man to man. Sixty-eight men became ill, and thirteen died. Soon after the cholera outbreak, the camp was disbanded, and the men were encouraged to return to their

---

18 Lucy Mack Smith, History, 1845, p. 221. Joseph Smith Papers.
19 Letter of Joseph Smith to Emma Smith, 18 May 1834, p. [1]. Spelling standardized. Joseph Smith Papers.
20 Letter of Joseph Smith to Emma Smith, 4 June 1834, pp. 57–58. Spelling standardized. Joseph Smith Papers.

families. When Joseph returned to Emma after walking "most of the [way to Missouri] and had a full proportion of blistered, bloody, and sore feet," he was charged "with a catalogue of charges as black as the author of lies himself." Cries of "Tyrant—Pope—King—Usurper—Abuser of men" were shouted in a spirit of contention and apostasy.[21] Acquitted of any wrongdoing, Joseph forgave his accusers and went about his work. The acquittal did not appease angry apostates, and they soon aligned themselves with the mob element in Kirtland.

Patriarchal Blessings

Amid a firestorm of malcontents in Kirtland, there was one night—the evening of December 9, 1834—when Joseph Smith Sr. gave patriarchal blessings to family members. Emma was told in her blessing,

> Emma, my daughter-in-law, thou art blessed of the Lord, for thy faithfulness and truth: thou shalt be blessed with thy husband and rejoice in the glory which shall come upon him: Thy soul has been afflicted because of the wickedness of men in seeking the destruction of thy companion, and thy whole soul has been drawn out in prayer for his deliverance: rejoice, for the Lord thy God has heard thy sup[p]lication. Thou hast grieved for the hardness of the hearts of thy father's house, and thou hast longed for their salvation. The Lord will have respect to thy cries, and by his judgments he will cause some of them to see their folly and repent of their sins; but it will be by affliction that they will be saved. Thou shall see many days; yea, the Lord will spare thee till thou are satisfied, for thou shalt see thy Redeemer. Thy heart shall rejoice in the great work of the Lord, and no one shall take thy rejoicing from thee.
>
> Thou shalt ever remember the great condescension of thy God in permitting thee to accompany my son when the angel delivered the record of the Nephites to his care. Thou hast seen much sorrow because the Lord has taken from thee three of thy children: in this thou art not to be blamed, for he knows thy pure desires to raise up a family, that the name of my son might be blessed. And now, behold, I say unto thee, that thus says the Lord, if thou will believe, thou shalt yet be blessed in this thing and thou shalt bring forth other children, to the

---

21 Journal of George A. Smith, June 25, 1834. Joseph Smith Papers.

joy and satisfaction of thy soul, and to the rejoicing of thy friends. Thou shalt be blessed with understanding, and have power to instruct thy sex. Teach thy family righteousness, and thy little ones the way of life, and the holy angels shall watch over thee: and thou shalt be saved in the kingdom of God; even so, Amen.[22]

The patriarchal blessings given to family members, like Emma, gave the Smiths hope and a sense of peace in what was a tumultuous time in their lives. Although the firestorm of naysayers could hardly be kept at bay, the Smiths were confident that God was mindful of their extremities and His loving care was extended to them.

Hymnbook

On September 14, 1835, the Kirtland High Council and Presidency of the Church resolved that "Sister Emma Smith proceed . . . to make a selection of sacred hymns, according to the Revelation, and that President W[illiam] W. Phelps be appointed to revise and arrange them for printing."[23] With the help of Phelps, Emma compiled the first hymnbook of the Church. Phelps contributed twenty-six hymns to *A Collection of Sacred Hymns, for the Church of the Latter Day Saints.* Selected by Emma Smith. Kirtland, Ohio: Printed by F. G. Williams & Co. 1835. The total number of hymns in the hymnal was ninety, the first being "Know Then That Ev'ry Soul Is Free" and the last "The Spirit of God like a Fire is Burning." The small, pocket-size hymnal was bound in leather and available for purchase in early February 1836. Many hymns included in the original hymnal appear in subsequent editions of the hymnal, giving Latter-day Saints today an opportunity to sing the hymns of Zion selected by Emma Smith.

Kirtland Temple Dedication

When construction on the Kirtland Temple was finished, "there was much rejoicing in the church, and great blessings poured out upon the Elders."[24] In

---

22 Patriarchal Blessing given to Emma Smith by Joseph Smith Sr., December 9, 1834, Kirtland Ohio, as transcribed by Oliver Cowdery. Patriarchal Blessing Book, 1:4-5, Church History Library; See "Patriarchal Blessing of Emma Smith," in H. Michael Marquardt, comp., *Early Patriarchal Blessings of the Church of Jesus Christ of Latter-day Saints* (Salt Lake City: The Smith-Pettit Foundation, 2007), p. 15.

23 History, 1838–1856, volume B-1 [1 September 1834–2 November 1838], p. 612 (14 September 1835). Joseph Smith Papers.

24 Lucy Mack Smith, History, 1845, ch. 45, p. 233. Joseph Smith Papers.

the temple dedicatory prayer, the Prophet Joseph petitioned the Lord, "And we ask thee, Holy Father, that thy servants may go forth from this house armed with thy power, and that thy name may be upon them, and thy glory be round about them . . . [Wilt thou] enable thy servants to seal up the law, and bind up the testimony" (D&C 109:22, 46). Convert Benjamin Brown heard the dedicatory prayer and testified to the fulfillment of Joseph's petition. "The Spirit of the Lord, as on the day of Pentecost, was profusely poured out. . . . Hundreds of Elders spoke in tongues. . . . We had a most glorious and never-to-be-forgotten time. Angels were seen by numbers present."[25]

A few months following the temple dedication, Emma gave birth to Frederick Granger Williams Smith on June 20, 1836. (The newborn was named for Joseph's counselor in the First Presidency—Frederick Granger Williams.) Unfortunately, neither Joseph nor Emma had much time to bask in the joy of his birth, for "it seemed as though all the powers of earth and hell were combining their influence in an especial manner to overthrow the Church at once, and make a final end." The persecution against Joseph became so violent that he "regarded it as unsafe to remain any longer in Kirtland and began to make arrangements to move [his family] to Missouri."[26]

In many ways, it was difficult for Emma to move again. She had spent nearly seven years in Ohio, buried three children, given birth to two children, and helped adorn a temple of God. Yet she was willing to follow her husband and the counsel of the Lord. With three young children to care for—Julia, Joseph, and baby Frederick—Emma fled from Kirtland to Far West, Missouri.

---

25   Benjamin Brown, *Testimonies for the Truth* (Liverpool: S. W. Richards, 1853), pp. 10–11.
26   Lucy Mack Smith, History, 1845, Document Transcript, ch. 47. Joseph Smith Papers.

Chapter Four

THE TRIBULATIONS OF MISSOURI

AT THE VERY TIME KIRTLAND was reeling with apostasy, the once faithful of Missouri were following the same forbidden path. Disaffected Saints from Kirtland had journeyed eight hundred miles "and contaminated the minds of many of the brethren [in Missouri] against Joseph, in order to destroy his influence."[1] Unfortunately, they found receptive listeners. Among the disaffected was Oliver Cowdery, who said, "Give me my freedom or take my life! I shall no longer be bound by the chains of hell. I shall speak out when I see a move to deceive the ignorant."[2] David Whitmer falsely claimed that Joseph had led the Saints to drift "into error and spiritual blindness."[3] (In November 1848, Oliver Cowdery appeared before the high council at Kanesville, Iowa, and formally requested fellowship in the Church. After his case was considered, and upon the motion of Orson Hyde, he was received by baptism. David Whitmer died outside the faith in 1888 in Richmond, Missouri, having never denied his testimony of the Book of Mormon.) As slanderous hearsay spread, attempts to establish truth were summarily dismissed as falsehoods. Solomon Hancock's unwavering testimony, "Br[other] Joseph is not a fallen prophet, but will yet be exalted and become very high," went almost unnoticed in an atmosphere of vexatious lawsuits, name-calling, and betrayal.[4]

Extermination Order

As apostates joined their cry of "fallen prophet" with shouts of "traitor," letters to Missouri civil leaders "begging their assistance against the 'Mormons'"

---

1   Lucy Mack Smith, History, 1845, p. 237. Joseph Smith Papers.
2   Huntington Library Letters, microfilm no. 87, as cited in Stanley R. Gunn, *Oliver Cowdery, Second Elder and Scribe* (Salt Lake City: Bookcraft, 1962), p. 230.
3   David Whitmer, *An Address to All Believers in Christ* (Richmond, MO: n.p. 1887), p. 59.
4   History, 1838–1856, volume C-1 [2 November 1838–31 July 1842], p. 867, Joseph Smith Papers.

proliferated. One letter stated that "Joseph Smith had himself killed seven men . . . and that the inhabitants had every reason to expect that he would collect his people together, as soon as possible, and murder all that did not belong to his church."[5] Believing the written falsehoods to be true and the escalating rumors to be valid, the governor of Missouri, Lilburn W. Boggs, called to arms the Missouri militia with orders to exterminate the Latter-day Saints or drive them from the state.

The Haun's Mill Massacre and the fall of Adam-ondi-Ahman were outgrowths of the government-sanctioned order to exterminate the Latter-day Saints. Frightened followers of Joseph Smith were subjected to the glitter of steel and the sheen of muskets as town after town fell to the Missouri militia. Hyrum Smith "endeavored to find out for what cause" the Latter-day Saints were being subjected to death. "All we could learn was, that it was because we were 'Mormons.'"[6]

Atrocities against the followers of Joseph Smith were unwarranted and cruel. Samuel Bent was tied to a tree and whipped by a mob.[7] Simeon Carter was wounded in a battle and "still determined to persevere and act in righteousness in all things so that he might at last gain a crown of glory."[8] David Fullmer "had a severe sickness and was reduced nigh unto death. Before he recovered, the mob came and order us to leave our homes and go away in twenty-four hours or they would come and burn our homes and destroy our property."[9]

In the days of such cruel persecution, Emma gave birth to Alexander Hale Smith on June 2, 1838, in her home at Far West. When Alexander was only five months old, his father, Joseph Smith, saw no alternative but to put himself and other Latter-day Saint leaders into the hands of the militia leaders or watch as the city of Far West was attacked and residents massacred. On October 31, 1838, Joseph, his brother Hyrum, Sidney Rigdon, Parley P. Pratt, and a few other Church leaders commended themselves to the Lord and voluntarily surrendered to the menacing militia "as sheep into the hands of wolves."[10]

As word spread through the militia camp of the surrender of Joseph Smith, militia soldiers yelled, "like so many bloodhounds let loose upon their prey. If the vision of the infernal regions could suddenly open to the mind, with thousands

---

5   Lucy Mack Smith, History, 1845, pgs. 247–248. Joseph Smith Papers.
6   Affidavits of Hyrum Smith et al. On Affairs in Missouri, 1831–39; Officially Subscribed to before the Municipal Court of Nauvoo The First Day of July 1843.
7   Donald Q. Cannon and Lyndon W. Cook ed., *Far West Record: Minutes of The Church of Jesus Christ of Latter-day Saints, 1833-1838* (Salt Lake City: Deseret Book, 1983), p. 222.
8   History, 1838–1856, volume C-1 [2 November 1838–31 July 1842], p. 867, Joseph Smith Papers.
9   "Experiences in the Life of Rhoda Ann Fullmer," n.p., n.d., p. 1. In author's possession.
10 Scot Facer Proctor and Maurine Jensen Proctor, *Autobiography of Parley P. Pratt: Revised and Enhanced Edition* (Salt Lake City: Deseret Book, 2000), pp. 234–35.

of malicious fiends, all clamoring . . . raging and foaming like a troubled sea, then could some idea be formed of the hell which we had entered."[11] When Father Smith heard the guns discharge in the militia encampment, he cried, "Oh My God! My God! they have murdered my Son and I must die for I cannot live without him."[12]

"A Prisoner for Christ's Sake"

Throughout the evening hours of October 31, 1838, the militia guards "kept up a constant tirade of mockery, and the most obscene blackguardism and abuse against their Latter-day Saint prisoners. They blasphemed God; mocked Jesus Christ; swore the most dreadful oaths and taunted Brother Joseph."[13] On November 1, a court-martial was held to determine the fate of Joseph and fellow captives. Fourteen officers, twenty preachers, and a few local judges were present at the court proceedings. When the court ended near midnight, General Samuel Lucas ordered General Alexander Doniphan to "execute the prisoners." Doniphan refused to comply.

Doniphan's defiance so alarmed General Lucas that he dared not execute the order. Rather than free the prisoners, he forced them to climb into wagons and prepare themselves for a journey to Independence. A request by the prisoners to bid their families farewell and obtain a change of clothing was reluctantly granted.

A guard of six men accompanied Joseph Smith into his home at Far West. Joseph Smith III recalled,

> I remember vividly the morning my father came to visit his family after the arrest [outside of Far West] . . . When he was brought to the house by an armed guard I ran out of the gate to greet him, but was roughly pushed away from his side by a sword in the hand of the guard and not allowed to go near him . . . My mother, also, was not permitted to approach him and had to receive his farewell by word of lip only. The guard did not permit him to pass into the house nor her to pass out.[14]

Another account of the same incident says that when six-year-old Joseph III asked, "Father, is the mob going to kill you?" a guard pushed the boy aside and said, "You damed little brat, go back, you will see your father no more."[15]

---

11 Ibid., p. 235.
12 Lucy Mack Smith, History, 1844–1845, bk. 16. Joseph Smith Papers.
13 Proctor and Proctor, *Autobiography of Parley P. Pratt*, p. 235.
14 Statement of Joseph Smith III, quoted in Mary Audentia Smith Anderson and Bertha Ardentia Anderson Hulmes, eds., *Joseph III and the Restoration* (Independence, MO.: Herald Publishing House, 1952), p. 2.
15 History, 1838–1856, volume D-1 [1 August 1842–1 July 1843], p. 1636. Joseph Smith Papers.

As Joseph left his home in Far West, he was shoved back into a prisoners' wagon. His guards then drove the wagon away from the city toward Independence. When they arrived in Independence, Church leaders were imprisoned in a vacant house and placed under military guard. It was then that Joseph wrote to Emma on November 4, 1838.

> My dear and beloved companion, on my bosom, in tribulation and affliction.
>
> I would inform you that I am well, and that we are all of us in good spirits as regards our own fate . . . I have great anxiety about you, and my lovely children, my heart morns [and] bleeds for the brothren [sic], and sisters, and for the slain [of the] people of God . . . those little [childrens] are subjects of my meditation continually, tell them that Father is yet alive, God grant that he may see them again Oh Emma for God sake do not forsake me nor the truth but remember, if I do [not] meet you again in this life may God grant that we may meet in heaven, I cannot express my feelings, my heart is full, Farewell Oh my kind and affectionate Emma I am yours forever your Husband and true friend.
>
> Joseph Smith Jr.[16]

Eight days later, on November 12, 1838, Joseph again wrote to Emma. This time, he was confined in a ramshackle log cabin in Richmond, Missouri.

> My Dear Emma.
>
> We are prisoners in chains, and under strong guards, for Christ's sake and for no other causes. . . . I received your letter which I read over and over again, it was a sweet morsel to me, Oh God grant that I may have the privilege of seeing once more my lovely Family, in the enjoyment, of the sweets of liberty, and societal life, to press them to my bosom and kiss their lovely cheeks would fill my heart with unspeakable gratitude, tell the children that I am alive and trust I shall come and see them before long, comfort their hearts all you can, and try to be comforted yourself, all you can . . . Oh my affectionate Emma, I want you to remember that I am [a] true and faithful friend, to you and the children, forever, my heart is entwined around yours forever and ever, Oh may God bless you all amen

---

16 Joseph Smith to Emma Smith, November 4, 1838. Spelling standardized. Church History Library; Letter to Emma Smith, 4 November 1838, pgs. 1–3. Joseph Smith Papers.

I am your husband and am in bonds and tribulations &c –
Joseph Smith Jr.
P S write as often as you can, and if possible come and see me, and bring the children if possible.[17]

From November 12 to November 29, 1838, Judge Austin A. King listened as alleged evidence was presented against Joseph and the other Latter-day Saint prisoners in a "court of inquiry" in Richmond, Missouri. At the end of what Hyrum Smith referred to as the "pretend court," Judge King found probable cause of treason against Joseph and five other prisoners and ordered these prisoners be transported to and confined in Liberty Jail.

On December 1, 1838, Joseph entered Liberty Jail. After the heavy door of the jail "swung upon its strong hinges" and closed, he sat down to write a brief letter to Emma—

My Dear companion I take this opportunity to inform you that we arrived in Liberty and committed to jail this Evening but we are all in good spirits Captain bogard [Samuel Bogart] will hand you this line my respects to all remain where you are at present
Yours &c—
—Joseph Smith Jr.[18]

The next week on December 8, Emma visited Joseph in Liberty Jail. She remained with him through the night and departed the next day.

Emma Flees from Missouri

The same winter that Joseph Smith was confined in Liberty Jail, Emma had her house ransacked: "A trunk stood open with its contents strewn about, a gold ring gone, and a sealed letter opened. A roll of linen cloth, some valuable buttons, a piece of cashmere and a number of prized books were missing."[19] John Lowe Butler's journal revealed the name of one culprit: "[William McLellin] went into brother Joseph's house and commenced searching over his things and Sister Emma asked him why he [had] done so." McLellin answered "Because I can." Butler wrote, "[McLellin] took all his jewelry out of Joseph's box and took a lot of his cloths and in fact, plundered the house and took the things off."[20]

---

17 Letter of Joseph Smith to Emma Smith, 12 November 1838, pgs. 1–2. Spelling standardized. Joseph Smith Papers.
18 Letter of Joseph Smith to Emma Smith, 1 December 1838, p. [1]. Spelling standardized. Joseph Smith Papers.
19 Newell and Avery, *Mormon Enigma: Emma Hale Smith*, p. 77.
20 Journal of John Lowe Butler, p. 20, as cited in Newell and Avery, *Mormon Enigma: Emma Hale Smith*, p. 77.

On February 7, 1839, Emma and her children fled from their home in Far West. With a friend driving her team and caring for her horses, Emma joined other religious exiles journeying from Far West to the banks of the Mississippi River, a distance of nearly two hundred miles. When she reached the Mississippi, Emma camped with her children across the river from Quincy, a fledgling town of about sixteen hundred settlers—mostly natives of New England. It was not the settlers of Quincy nor the picturesque setting of the city on the limestone bluff that caused Latter-day Saints like Emma to gather across from Quincy. It was the ferryboat facilities in Quincy Bay that attracted the exiles. They hoped that rivercraft would transport them away from the dangers in Missouri to safety on Illinois shores.

Unfortunately, floating ice on the Mississippi delayed most rivercrafts from conveying the religious exiles to safety. The "ice had broken up on the west side of the river and was running so the ferry boat could not cross," Sarah Rich wrote. "All chance for crossing was to go across in a skiff or canoe through the ice until they reached the island and from there walk on the ice to reach Quincy on the east side."[21]

Among the refugees waiting to cross the icy river was Lucy Mack Smith. She wrote,

> The snow was now six inches deep and still falling—we made our beds upon it and went to rest, with what comfort we might under such circumstances. The next morning our beds were covered with snow, and much of the bedding under which we lay, frozen. We rose and tried to light a fire; but finding it impossible, we resigned ourselves to our comfortless situation.[22]

Some Latter-day Saints, anxious to escape further suffering in the frigid winter, attempted to cross the river in canoes, "paddling through the ice, the women holding onto the side while the floating ice cut their fingers."[23] Others waited for a more opportune crossing, believing it would be when the river froze over. When the river did freeze over, Latter-day Saints crossed on the ice to Quincy. Numbered among those walking across the frozen river was Emma Smith. On February 15, 1839, with two babies—Alexander and Frederick—in her arms and two children—Joseph and Julia—at her skirts, Emma walked across the frozen Mississippi to safety in Quincy, Illinois. In cotton bags under

---

21 Sarah Rich Autobiography, typescript 29–30. L. Tom Perry Special Collections, Harold B. Lee Library, Brigham Young University, Provo, UT.
22 Lucy Mack Smith, History, 1845, pgs. 286–287. Joseph Smith Papers.
23 *Latter-day Saint Biographical Encyclopedia*, p. 205.

her dress, Emma carried Joseph's private papers and the manuscript of his inspired translation of the Bible.

Attorney Orville H. Browning witnessed Latter-day Saint exiles, like Emma and her children, cross the river on the frozen ice: "Great God! have I not seen it? Yes, my eyes have beheld the bloodstained traces of innocent women and children, in the drear winter, who had travelled hundreds of miles barefoot, through frost and snow, to seek a refuge from their savage pursuers. 'Twas a scene of horror, sufficient to enlist sympathy from an adamantine heart."[24] Quincy residents compassionately cared for Emma and her children and other Latter-day Saint refugees as one would care for an enduring friend. Quincyans offered hearth and home, sustenance and possessions, to provide much-needed relief to the exiles.

On March 7, 1839 Emma wrote to Joseph—

> I shall not attempt to write my feelings altogether, for the situation in which you are, the walls, bars, and bolts, rolling rivers, running streams, rising hills, sinking valleys and spreading prairies that separate us, and the cruel injustice that first cast you into prison and still holds you there, with many other considerations, places my feelings far beyond description. Were it not for conscious innocence, and the direct interposition of divine mercy, I am very sure I never should have been able to have endured the scenes of suffering that I have passed through, since what is called the Militia, came in to Far West, under the ever to be remembered Governor's notable order . . .
>
> No one but God, knows the reflections of my mind and the feelings of my heart when I left our house and home, and almost all of every thing that we possessed excepting our little Children, and took my journey out of the State of Missouri, leaving you shut up in that lonesome prison. But the recollection is more than human nature ought to bear . . . I have many more things I could like to write but have not time and you may be astonished at my bad writing and incoherent manner, but you will pardon all when you reflect how hard it would be for you to write, when your hands are stiffened with hard work, and your heart convulsed with intense anxiety. But I hope there is better days to come to us yet.[25]

---

24 History, 1838–1856, volume C-1 [2 November 1838–31 July 1842], p. 1207. Joseph Smith Papers.
25 Letter of Emma Smith to Joseph Smith, 7 March 1839, p. 37. Spelling standardized. Joseph Smith Papers.

On March 21, 1839 from Liberty Jail, Joseph penned:

> Affectionate Wife . . .
>
> Dear Emma I very well know your toils and sympathize with you if God will spare my life once more to have the privilege of taking care of you I will ease your care and endeavor to comfort your heart . . . Dear Emma do you think that my being cast into prison by the mob renders me less worthy of your friendship no I do not think so but when I was in prison and ye visited me inasmuch as you have done it to the least [of] these you have done it to me these shall enter into life Eternal but no more
>
> your Husband.[26]

In his last letter from Liberty Jail, Joseph penned on April 4, 1839—

> Dear—and affectionate—Wife
>
> Thursday night I sat down just as the sun is going down, as we peak through the grates of this lonesome prison, to write to you, that I may make known to you my situation. It is I believe now about five months and six days since I have been under the grimace, of a guard night and day, and within the walls grates and screeching iron doors, of a lonesome dark dirty prison. . . . My Dear Emma I think of you and the children continually. . . . as to yourself if you want to know how much I want to see you, examine your feelings, how much you want to see me, and judge for [yourself], I would gladly [walk] from here to you barefoot, and bareheaded, and half naked, to see you and think it great pleasure.
>
> —[Joseph Smith Jr.][27]

Joseph and the other Latter-day Saint prisoners were taken from Liberty Jail to Gallatin, Missouri, on April 6, 1839, never to return to the loathsome prison again. Before many days had passed, Joseph had escaped from his captors and had joined Emma and his children in Quincy.

---

26 Letter of Joseph Smith to Emma Smith, 21 March 1839, pgs. [1 & 3]. Spelling standardized. Joseph Smith Papers.

27 Letter of Joseph Smith to Emma Smith, 4 April 1839, p. [1]. Spelling standardized. Joseph Smith Papers.

Chapter Five

AN ELECT LADY

IN 1839, SPECULATORS SCURRIED TO find buyers for investments gone sour in the swamplands of Illinois. They offered to sell the infested marshland of Commerce for almost no money down. Latter-day Saint exiles from Missouri could afford little more, and so the purchase price for the swamp was agreed upon. In describing the purchase, Joseph Smith said, "The place was literally a wilderness. The land was mostly covered with trees and bushes, and much of it so wet that it was with the utmost difficulty a foot man could get through, and totally impossible for teams." Yet with "no more eligible place, presenting itself," the Prophet Joseph "considered it wisdom to make an attempt to build up a City."[1]

Following the advice of the Prophet Joseph, his followers moved to Commerce. Weakened by their ordeals in Missouri and living in makeshift tents and wagons in the swamp-laden community, thousands of Saints fell prey to illnesses inherent in the Mississippi valley. "It was a very sickly time," wrote Wilford Woodruff. "Joseph had given up his home in Commerce to the sick, and had a tent pitched in his dooryard and was living in that himself."[2]

Lucy Mack Smith was among those who suffered from the "strange fever" that infested the marshy lowlands. "I was taken [very] sick and was brought nigh unto death," she recalled. "For five nights Emma never left me; but stood at my bed side all the night long. At the end of which time she was overcome with fatigue and was taken sick herself." Mother Smith continued, "Joseph then took her place, and watched with me the five succeeding nights, as faithfully

---

1   History, 1838–1856, volume C-1 [2 November 1838–31 July 1842], p. 954 (11 June 1839). Joseph Smith Papers.
2   Wilford Woodruff, Journal, May 1839, as cited in Matthias Cowley, *Wilford Woodruff, History of His Life and Labors* (Salt Lake City: Bookcraft, 1964), p. 104. See also Wilford Woodruff, Journals and Papers 1828–1898, Church History Library.

as Emma had done."[3] With illness and death on every side, Joseph questioned whether he too would succumb. He sought the answer from his father. "You shall even live to finish your work," his father promised him. Joseph cried out, "Oh my father will I?" His father answered, "Yes, you shall live to lay out the plan of all the work which God has given you to do."[4]

Joseph, relieved by the patriarchal assurance, went forward with confidence. For a brief season, the people of Commerce and their Prophet saw "sickness cease from among us, and the mob retire to their homes," and the fledgling city become a haven.[5] With hammer, saw, trowel, and shovel, Latter-day Saints replaced the squalor of makeshift tents and log cottages with permanent structures. Home and shop next to barn and stable, with a family garden in between, became the norm. Joseph told settlers along the Mississippi that he "would build up a City, and the old inhabitants replied 'we will be damned if you can' So I prophesied that I would build up a City, and the Inhabitants prophesied I could not."[6]

Nauvoo—The City Beautiful

Joseph's city became known as "Nauvoo—The City Beautiful." There the Latter-day Saints built gristmills, lumber mills, potteries, tanneries, brickyards, bakeries, and dozens of other home industries. Prosperity could be seen on every hand in the city. The housing market boomed, and in the prairie lands east of Nauvoo were planted fields of golden grain. Joseph and Emma would have enjoyed more of the prosperity in Nauvoo had it not been for their unchecked charity: "My house has been a home and resting place for thousands," wrote Joseph, "and my family many times obliged to do without food, after having fed all they had to visitors."[7] William W. Phelps suggested that Joseph "must do as [Napoleon] Bonaparte did, have a little table, just large enough for the victuals you want yourself." Emma replied, "Mr. Smith is a bigger man than Bonaparte, he can never eat without his 'friends.'"[8]

The Prophet Joseph often assisted Emma with the task of feeding visitors and caring for her in times of sickness. At a party held in their home, "twenty

---

3   Lucy Mack Smith, History, 1845, p. 306. Joseph Smith Papers.
4   Lucy Mack Smith, History, 1845, p. 298. Joseph Smith Papers.
5   History, 1838–1856, volume E-1 [1 July 1843–30 April 1844], p. 1869. Joseph Smith Papers; Lucy Mack Smith, History, 1845, p. 304. Joseph Smith Papers.
6   History, 1838–1856, volume D-1 [1 August 1842–1 July 1843], Document Transcript, p. 1443 (5 January 1843). Spelling standardized. Joseph Smith Papers.
7   History, 1838–1856, volume E-1 [1 July 1843–30 April 1844], p. 1734 (15 September 1843). Joseph Smith Papers.
8   History, 1838–1856, volume E-1 [1 July 1843–30 April 1844], p. 1853, (4 January 1844). Joseph Smith Papers; see also Gracia Lorena Normandeau Jones, *Priceless Gifts: Celebrating the Holidays with Joseph and Emma* (American Fork, UT: Covenant Communications, 1998).

one [guests] sat down to the dinner table, and Emma and myself waited on them," Joseph wrote.[9] "Emma began to be sick with fever, consequently I kept in the house with her all day," was penned in a journal entry.[10] When a Latter-day Saint observed Joseph doing "woman's work," he, Jesse Crosby, erroneously concluded that Emma's mismanagement of the home was the root of a domestic problem. "I said to him, 'Brother Joseph, my wife does much more hard work than does your wife.'" The Prophet replied, "If a man cannot learn in this life to appreciate a wife and do his duty by her, in properly taking care of her, he need not expect to be given one in the hereafter." The judgmental advisor wrote, "His words shut my mouth as tight as a clam. I took them as terrible reproof. After that I tried to do better by the good wife I had and tried to lighten her labors."[11]

Joseph's tenderness toward Emma in her times of need was characteristic of his kindness to others. When he learned that a member of the Church had lost his home to a raging fire, Joseph reached into his pocket, pulled out a five-dollar coin, and said, "I feel sorry for this brother to the amount of five dollars; how much do you feel sorry?"[12]

Second Hymnbook

Prayer and song was a nightly tradition in Joseph and Emma's home. "I arrived at [Joseph's] house about nine o'clock, just as his family was singing, before the accustomed evening prayer," penned William Holmes Walker. "[Joseph's] wife Emma, leading in the singing. I thought I had never heard such a sweet, heavenly music before."[13] Perhaps it was her singing voice, but more likely, the revelation received in July 1830 was the reason why Emma was asked to compile a second hymnal. Either way, on October 27, 1839, the High Council of Nauvoo "voted, that Sister Emma Smith select and publish a Hymn Book for the use of the Church, and that Brigham Young be informed of the same, and he not publish the Hymns taken by him from Commerce [to England]; and that

---

9   History, 1838–1856, volume D-1 [1 August 1842–1 July 1843], p. 1455, (18 January 1843). Joseph Smith Papers.
10 History, 1838–1856, volume D-1 [1 August 1842–1 July 1843], Document Transcript, (29 September 1842). Joseph Smith Papers.
11 Hyrum L. Andrus and Helen Mae Andrus, *They Knew the Prophet* (Salt Lake City: Deseret Book, 1999), p. 164.
12 Edwin F. Parry, comp., *Stories about Joseph Smith the Prophet*, p. 22, as citied in *Teachings of the Presidents of the Church: Joseph Smith*, Chapter 40.
13 William Holmes Walker, *The Life Incidents and Travels of Elder William Holmes Walker and his Association with Joseph Smith, the Prophet*, p. 8, as cited in Newell and Avery, *Mormon Enigma*, p. 89.

the Council assist in publishing a Hymn Book and the *Times and Seasons*."[14] In accordance with the vote, Emma compiled a second hymnal, which included 304 hymns with suggested tempos. Much controversy arose at this time over Emma's hymnal and Brigham Young printing a hymnal in England, which led to a rift between Emma and Brigham.

Birth and Death of Don Carlos Smith

On June 13, 1840, Emma gave birth to her sixth son—Don Carlos Smith, named after Joseph's brother. The child's death on August 15, 1841, was devastating to Joseph and Emma. Many years later, in a dream shortly before her own death, Emma saw herself being taken by Joseph into a heavenly mansion and shown about from room to room. "One room was the nursery. In that nursery was a babe in the cradle. . . . I knew my babe, my Don Carlos that was taken from me." In the dream, Emma caught the child up in her arms and wept for joy. After a moment, she asked Joseph, "Where are the rest of my children?" He replied, "Emma be patient and you shall have all of your children."[15] On February 6, 1842, Emma delivered a stillborn son.

The Female Relief Society of Nauvoo

Sarah Melissa Kimball, wife of Hiram Kimball, and her seamstress, Miss Cook, wanted to help the poor of Nauvoo. Sarah wrote, "I told [Miss Cook] I would furnish material if she would make some shirts for the workman" in the temple quarries. The two women reached an agreement and went to work. As Sarah recalled, "We decided to invite a few to come and consult with us on the subject of forming a Ladies' Society to help the poor of Nauvoo. The neighboring sisters met in my parlor and decided to organize" on March 4, 1842.[16]

To be fully organized like other benevolent societies in the Midwestern states, the Ladies' Society needed a constitution and an election of officers. Sarah Kimball asked Eliza R. Snow to create the constitution and bylaws for the society before elections were held. Eliza wrote the documents and showed her work to Joseph Smith, who remarked that the "Constitution and Bylaws were the best he had ever seen." However, Joseph told Eliza that the Lord wanted to provide "something better for [the women of Nauvoo] than a written Constitution." Joseph said, "I will organize the women under the priesthood after the pattern of the priesthood."[17]

---

14 "History of Joseph Smith," *Latter-day Saints' Millennial Star* 17 (1855): 372.
15 In the final days of Emma's life her son Alexander recorded that she had a remarkable dream. In Gracia N. Jones, "My Great-Great Grandmother, Emma Hale Smith," *Ensign*, August 1992.
16 Kimball, "Auto-biography," *Woman's Exponent* 12, no. 7 (September 1, 1883): 51.
17 Kimball, "Auto-biography," *Woman's Exponent* 12, no. 7 (September 1, 1883): 51.

On Thursday, March 17, 1842, Joseph organized the Female Relief Society of Nauvoo. Thirty-eight-year-old Emma Smith was elected president of the society. The purpose of the society was not to follow the "popular Institutions of the day" but to "set an example for all the world."[18]

> *The Female Relief Society of Nauvoo*
> What is it?
> It is an Institution form'd to bless
> The poor, the widow, and the fatherless—
> To clothe the naked and the hungry feed,
> And in the holy paths of virtue, lead.
>
> To seek out sorrow, grief and mute despair,
> And light the lamp of hope eternal there—
> To try the strength of consolation's art
> By breathing comfort to the mourning heart.
>
> To chase the clouds that shade the aspect, where
> Distress presides; and wake up pleasures there—
> With open heart extend the friendly hand
> To hail the stranger, from a distant land.
>
> To stamp a vetoing impress on each move
> That Virtue's present dictates disapprove—
> To put the tattler's coinage, scandal, down,
> And make corruption feel its with'ring frown.
>
> To give instruction, where instruction's voice
> Will guide the feet and make the heart rejoice—
> To turn the wayward from their recklessness,
> And lead them in the ways of happiness.
>
> It is an *Order*, fitted and design'd
> To meet the wants of body, and of mind—
> To seek the wretched, in their long abode—
> Supply their wants, and raise their hearts to God.
> —E. R. Snow[19]

---

18 Relief Society Minute Book, March 1842–March 1844, March 17, 1842. Church History Library.
19 E. R. Snow, "The Female Relief Society of Nauvoo—What is it?" *Times and Seasons* 3, no. 17 (July 1, 1842): 846.

Joseph said to the women, "I now turn the key in your behalf in the name of the Lord, and this society shall rejoice and knowledge and intelligence shall flow down from this time henceforth."[20] He challenged the society to search out the needy and minister to their needs. "This is . . . according to your natures," he told the sisters.

> It is natural for females to have feelings of charity and benevolence you are now placed in a situation in which you can act according to those sympathies which God has planted in your bosoms. If you live up to these principles how great and glorious will be your reward in the celestial kingdom!! If you live up to your privileges the angels cannot be restrained from being your associates.[21]

He then said, "This is the beginning of better days to the poor and needy, who shall be made to rejoice and pour forth blessings on your heads."[22]

Emma remarked, "We are going to do something *extraordinary*—when a boat is stuck on the rapids, with a multitude of Mormons on board, we shall consider *that* a loud call for *relief*—we expect extraordinary occasions and pressing calls."[23] Instead of waiting for calls of distress, Emma encouraged the sisters of the society to search out those in need. She noted that Philindia Myrick, a widow caring for three children, was "industrious—performs her work well, [and] therefore recommend[ed] her to the patronage of such as wish to hire needlework."[24] Emma "hired a poor man to plough and fence father Knights lot at $.22,60, and solicited the Society in behalf of the payment which might be made in provision, clothing, and furniture."[25]

Under Emma's able guidance, heavy burdens were lifted, and necessities needed to sustain life were freely proffered. Employment was secured, temporary housing obtained, and clothing and provisions were provided to sustain life in Nauvoo. In July 1842, Emma Smith and a few sisters met with the governor of Illinois, Thomas Carlin. Eliza R. Snow reported:

---

20 History, 1838–1856, volume C-1 Addenda, p. 42. Joseph Smith Papers.
21 History, 1838–1856, volume C-1 Addenda, p. 40. Joseph Smith Papers; Relief Society Minute Book, March 1842–March 1844, March 17, 1842.
22 History, 1838–1856, volume C-1 Addenda, p. 42, Joseph Smith Papers.
23 Relief Society Minute Book, March 1842–March 1844, March 17, 1842, Church History Library.
24 Jill Mulvay Derr, Janath Russell Cannon, and Maureen Ursenbrach Beecher, *Women of Covenant: The Story of Relief Society* (Salt Lake City: Deseret Book, 1992), p. 31.
25 Relief Society Minute Book, March 1842–March 1844, May 27, 1842, Church History Library.

The governor received us with cordiality, and as much affability and politeness as his excellency is a master of, assuring us of his protection, by saying that the laws and constitution of our country shall be his polar star in case of any difficulty. He manifested much friendship, and it remains for time and circumstances to prove the sincerity of his profession.[26]

Joseph expressed gratitude to the society for taking a "most active part in my welfare against my enemies." He then said, "God loves you, and your prayers in my behalf shall avail much;—let them not cease to ascend to God continually in my behalf."[27] The Relief Society of The Church of Jesus Christ of Latter-day Saints continues to extend compassion to the world's downtrodden. From Africa to the Orient and from Europe to South America, the less fortunate are made glad by the thoughtful kindness of women in this society. Today, the Relief Society is one of the largest organizations of women in the world.

Joseph in Hiding

To escape from his enemies, Joseph went into hiding north of Nauvoo in the summer of 1842. He wrote to Emma on August 16, 1842:

My Dear Emma—

I embrace this opportunity to express to you some of my feelings this morning. First of all, I take the liberty to tender you my sincere thanks for the two interesting and consoling visits that you have made me during my almost exiled situation. Tongue can not express the gratitude of my heart, for the warm and true-hearted friendship you have manifested in these things toward me. The time has passed away since you left me, very agreeably; thus far, my mind being perfectly reconciled to my fate, let it be what it may. . . . I think if I could have a respite of about six months with my family, it would be a savor of life unto life . . . Tell the children that it is well with their father, as yet; and that he remains in fervent prayer to Almighty God for the safety of himself, and for you, and for them . . .

---

26 Relief Society Minute Book, March 1842–March 1844, April 19, 1842, Church History Library.
27 History, 1838–1856, volume D-1 [1 August 1842–1 July 1843], p. 2 [addenda], (31 August 1842), Joseph Smith Papers.

> Yours in haste, Your affectionate husband until death, through all eternity forevermore
> —Joseph Smith[28]

Emma wrote back the same day—

> Dear Husband:
> I am ready to go with you if you are obliged to leave; and Hyrum [Smith] says he will go with me. I shall make the best arrangements I can and be as well prepared as possible. But still I feel good confidence that you can be protected without leaving this country. . . .
> Yours affectionately forever
> Emma Smith[29]

In a reflective mood, Joseph dictated his sentiments about Emma to his clerk, William Clayton:

> With what unspeakable delight, and what transports of joy swelled my bosom, when I took by the hand on that night, my beloved Emma, she that was my wife, even the wife of my youth; and the choice of my heart. Many were the re-vibrations of my mind when I contemplated for a moment the many scenes we had been called to pass through. The fatigues, and the toils, the sorrows, and sufferings, and the joys and consolations from time to time had strewed our paths and crowned our board. Oh! what a comingling of thought filled my mind for the moment, Again she is here, even in the seventh trouble, undaunted, firm and unwavering, unchangeable, affectionate Emma.[30]

On August 17, 1842, Emma wrote to Illinois Governor Thomas Carlin, "Pleading the Cause of the Prophet and the People of Nauvoo." A portion of her letter reads, "My husband; who has not committed any crime whatever . . . [The charges against him] were the effect of unjust prejudice and misguided ambition,

---

28 Letter of Joseph Smith to Emma Smith, 16 August 1842, pp. 173–75, Joseph Smith Papers.
29 Letter of Emma Smith to Joseph Smith, 16 August 1842, p. 175, Joseph Smith Papers.
30 Journal, December 1841–December 1842, p. 164, Joseph Smith Papers.

produced by misrepresentation and calumny."[31] It was reported, "the Governor read the letter [from Emma] with much attention, apparently, and when he got through he passed high encomiums on Emma Smith, and expressed astonishment at the judgment and talent manifest in the manner of her address."[32] Within the month, Joseph had returned to Nauvoo.

Emma Becomes Very Ill

In late September 1842, Emma fell dangerously ill. Joseph feared that Emma might not recover. His brief journal entries express his concern: "Emma is no better, I was with her all day . . . Emma was a little better. I was with her all day . . . Emma was very sick again. I attended with her all the day being somewhat poorly myself."[33] On October 5, Joseph wrote, "My dear Emma was worse, many fears were entertained, that she would not recover."[34] The next day Joseph penned, "Emma is better, and although it is the day on which she generally grows worse, yet she appears considerably easier. May the Lord speedily raise her to the bosom of her family, that the heart of his servant may be comforted again. Amen."[35]

---

31 Journal, December 1841–December 1842, pgs. 176–77, (16 August 1842), Joseph Smith Papers.
32 History, 1838–1856, volume D-1 [1 August 1842–1 July 1843], Document Transcript, (19 August 1842), Joseph Smith Papers.
33 History, 1838–1856, volume D-1 [1 August 1842–1 July 1843], Document Transcript, (30 September, 3 October and 4 October 1842), Joseph Smith Papers.
34 History, 1838–1856, volume D-1 [1 August 1842–1 July 1843], Document Transcript, (5 October 1842), p. 1405. Joseph Smith Papers.
35 History, 1838–1856, volume D-1 [1 August 1842–1 July 1843], Document Transcript, (6 October 1842), Joseph Smith Papers.

Chapter Six

THE MARTYRDOM

The tentative peace in Nauvoo ended in 1843. Ridicule, arrest warrants, and evil speaking accelerated as apostates searched for ways to thwart the plans of God and malign the character of His Prophet. Doctrines declared sacred by Joseph were distorted to disprove his claims to divine revelation and arouse angry public sentiment to new heights. Unfounded rumors of a secret military invasion of Nauvoo to capture the Prophet Joseph were declared as truths.

To Church members and non-members alike, an open conflict between the city of Nauvoo and neighbors in outlying communities seemed the only solution to the escalating tension. Gun salesmen, believing conflict inevitable, tried to entice the Latter-day Saints to buy weapons to defend themselves against imminent danger. Joseph counseled the Saints not to buy weapons: "It would be better to buy plough shares and raise corn with them. . . . Let us keep cool as a cucumber on a frosty morning."[1]

Keeping cool was not easy, for Joseph's enemies were within the city. Yet Saints like Emma Smith went about their days as if the tentative calm would last a lifetime. Emma was sealed to the Prophet Joseph for all eternity. She performed proxy baptisms in the Mississippi River for her father, Isaac Hale, mother, Elizabeth Lewis Hale, sister Phebe Roote, aunt Esther Hale, uncle Reuben Hale, and great-aunt Eunice Cady.[2] She celebrated her thirty-ninth birthday by riding horses with Joseph out to their farm. Emma "was fond of horses and could manage them well in riding or driving," wrote Emmeline B. Wells. "Many

---

1   History, 1838–1856, volume E-1 [1 July 1843–30 April 1844], p. 1836, Joseph Smith Papers; *Smith History of the Church*, 6:151.
2   Nauvoo Baptismal Records of the Dead, Book A 45, 143, Book C 153. See also Susan Easton Black and Harvey Bischoff Black, *Annotated Record of Baptisms for the Dead, 1840-1845, Nauvoo, Hancock County, Illinois* 7 vols. (Provo, UT: The Center for Family History and Genealogy, Brigham Young University, 2002), 6:3354–56.

can recall seeing her mounted on horseback beside her husband in military parade and a grander couple could nowhere be found."³

In her thirty-ninth year, Emma hosted dignitaries, such as Judge Stephen A. Douglas, who was seeking political office and courting the Latter-day Saint vote. Emma served apple fritters to the delight of Douglas and other politically minded guests. When one guest asked the name of the morsel, Emma said, "I call it a candidate." "Why?" the man wanted to know. "Why not?" she answered. "Isn't it just a puff of wind?"⁴ Emma's confidence was high and would remain so for years to come.

At what could have been an enjoyable family outing at Emma's sister's house in Dixon, Illinois, Joseph was kidnapped by Sheriff J. H. Reynolds of Missouri and Harmon T. Wilson of Carthage. Rather than stay in Dixon and fret, Emma gathered her children and left immediately for Nauvoo. Soon after she arrived in the city, Joseph arrived also, much to the chagrin of his captors who had hoped to convey Joseph as their prisoner in Missouri.

Believing a sense of normalcy had returned, in September 1843, Joseph and his family moved into the Mansion House. Wanting furnishings to enhance the interior of the house, Emma went on a shopping spree in St. Louis. When she returned home, she found the Mansion House equipped with a bar, and Orin Porter Rockwell was the designated bartender. "Joseph, what is the meaning of that bar in this house?" Emma asked.

> How does it look for the spiritual head of a religious body to be keeping a hotel in which a room is fitted out as a liquor selling establishment? . . . I will take my children and go across to the old house and stay there, for I will not have them raised up under such conditions as this arrangement imposes upon us, nor have them mingle with the kind of men who frequent such a place. You are at liberty to make your choice; either that bar goes out of the house, or we will!

"Very well, Emma; I will have it removed at once," Joseph said.⁵

June 1844

By June 1844, Carthage was teaming with malcontents. Although tensions were heightened in Nauvoo, the Prophet Joseph remained calm. He was confident that "all the enemies upon the face of the earth may roar and exert all

---

3 Emmeline B. Wells, "L.D.S. Women of the Past," *Woman's Exponent* 36, no. 7 (February 1908): 490.
4 Vesta Crawford Notes, University of Utah, as cited in Newell and Avery, *Mormon Enigma: Emma Hale Smith*, pp. 178–179.
5 Newell and Avery, *Mormon Enigma: Emma Hale Smith*, pp. 178–179.

their power to bring about my death; but they can accomplish nothing, unless some who are among us and, enjoying our society . . . join with our enemies." He knew that his "life [was] more in danger from some little dough-head of a fool in this city, than from all my numerous and inveterate enemies abroad. I am exposed to far great danger from traitors among ourselves than from enemies without."6

Traitors within Nauvoo had bound themselves together in an oath of conspiracy: "You solemnly swear, before God and all holy angels, and these your brethren by whom you are surrounded, that you will give your life, your liberty, your influence, your all, for the destruction of Joseph Smith and his part, so help you God."7 Although Joseph believed the traitors "would not scare off an old setting hen," their evil plans ignited public sentiment to a feverish pitch when they printed the *Nauvoo Expositor*.8 The first and only issue of the *Expositor* charged Joseph with indulging in whoredoms and abusing political power. It branded him as a base seducer, liar, and murderer. One reader reported that editors of the *Expositor* "belched forth the most intolerable, and blackest lies that were ever palmed upon a community."9

As mayor of Nauvoo, Joseph met with the Nauvoo City Council to discuss the libelous accusations printed in the *Expositor*. The official decision stemming from the discussions was to denounce the newspaper as a public nuisance and authorize the Nauvoo sheriff to stop future publications. The swift, decisive actions of the sheriff and his posse led publishers of the *Expositor* to charge Joseph and the Nauvoo City Council with starting a riot that led to the demise of their newspaper.

The incident added fuel to the mounting prejudice and hatred of nearby neighbors. Thomas Sharp, editor of a small newspaper in Warsaw, Illinois, announced that "war and extermination is inevitable" against the Latter-day Saints of Nauvoo. He encouraged residents of Warsaw and Carthage to take up arms and destroy Nauvoo: "Citizens arise, one and all!!! Can you stand by, and suffer such infernal devils! to rob men of their property and rights, without avenging them. We have no time for comment, every man will make his own. Let it be made with powder and ball!!!"10

---

6   History, 1838–1856, volume E-1 [1 July 1843–30 April 1844], p. 1836, Joseph Smith Papers.
7   Horace Cummings, "Conspiracy of Nauvoo," *Contributor* 5 (April 1884): 255.
8   Discourse, 24 March 1844-A, as Reported by Wilford Woodruff, p. [214], Joseph Smith Papers.
9   Lucy Mack Smith, History, 1845, p. 309. Joseph Smith Papers.
10 *Warsaw Signal*, June 12, 1844; see Roger D. Launius, "Anti-Mormonism in Illinois: Thomas C. Sharp's Unfinished History of the Mormon War, 1845," *Journal of Mormon History* 15 (1989): 30.

The inescapable target of the proposed extermination was the Prophet Joseph. "Joe Smith, is not safe out of Nauvoo," trumpeted the *Warsaw Signal*. "We would not be surprised to hear of his death by violent means in a short time. He has deadly enemies. . . . The feeling in this county is now lashed to its utmost pitch, and will break forth in fury upon the slightest provocation."[11] To Joseph, such threats were appalling. "I will never tamely submit to the dominion of cursed mobocracy," he said. "I do not regard my own life—I am ready to be offered a sacrifice for this people; for what can our enemies do? only kill the body, and their power is then at an end."[12]

Attempting to escape from the mob element in Hancock County, Joseph and his brother Hyrum left Nauvoo on June 23 and crossed the Mississippi River to Iowa. On that date, Joseph wrote a hurried note to Emma about temporal affairs and concerns.

> Brother Lewis has some money of mine–H[eber] C. Kimball has $1000, in his hand of mine, Br Neff, Lancaster Co, Pa.,—$400, You may sell the Quincy Property. —or any property that belongs to me you can find anything about, for your support and children & Mother. Do not despair—If God ever opens a door that is possible for me I will see you again . . . God Almighty bless you & the children & Mother & all my friends.[13]

Ill-advised friends in Iowa encouraged Joseph and Hyrum to return to the Illinois side of the river, submit to the law, and face an arraignment in Carthage on the trumped-up charge of riot. Emma had the same inclination. She "sent over to O. P. Rockwell, requesting him to entreat of Joseph to come back [from Iowa]; Reynolds Cahoon accompanied [Rockwell] with a letter which Emma had written to the same effect, and she insisted that Cahoon should persuade Joseph to come back and give himself up."[14] Benjamin F. Johnson wrote in his journal, "Through the persuasion and reproaches of his wife, Emma, and others [Joseph] was induced to return and give himself up to the slaughter."[15] With resignation, Joseph said,

---

11 *Warsaw Signal*, May 29, 1844.
12 History, 1838–1856, volume F-1 [1 May 1844–8 August 1844], p. 119, Joseph Smith Papers; History, 1838–1856, volume D-1 [1 August 1842–1 July 1843], p. 6 [addenda], Joseph Smith Papers.
13 Letter of Joseph Smith to Emma Smith, 23 June 1844, p. [1]. Spelling standardized. Joseph Smith Papers.
14 History, 1838–1856, volume F-1 [1 May 1844–8 August 1844], p. 148. Spelling standardized. Joseph Smith Papers.
15 Benjamin F. Johnson, *My Life's Review* (Heber City, UT: Archive Publishers, 2001), 120.

If my life is of no value to my friends it is of none to myself... I am going like a lamb to the slaughter, but I am calm as a summer's morning; I have a conscience void of offence toward God, and toward all men; if they take my life I shall die an innocent man, and my blood shall cry from the ground for vengeance, and it shall be said of me "he was murdered in cold blood."[16]

When Joseph and Hyrum crossed over the Mississippi to Nauvoo, they were resigned to their fate: "If we live or have to die we will be reconciled."[17] They bid farewell to their families before beginning their final journey to Carthage. As Joseph gazed upon the city he had orchestrated, he said, "This is the loveliest place and the best people under the heavens; little do they know the trials that await them."[18]

Carthage

For Joseph and Hyrum, Carthage was a scene of broken promises, illegal arraignment, and incarceration. Accusations of riot stemming from the *Nauvoo Expositor* incident were turned to treason. Rumors once whispered in secret now were shouted. The militant unabashedly declared the Smith brothers would not leave Carthage: "There was nothing against these men; the law could not reach them, but powder and ball would, and they should not go out of Carthage alive."[19]

At 2:30 p.m. on June 25, 1844, Joseph wrote to Emma:

> Dear Emma—
> I have had an interview with Gov. [Thomas] Ford & he treats us honorably. Myself & Hyrum have been again arrested—for treason because we called out the Nauvoo Legion, but when the truth comes out we have nothing to fear: we all feel calm & composed....
> Governor Ford has just concluded to send some of his militia to Nauvoo to protect the citizens....

---

16 History, 1838–1856, volume F-1 [1 May 1844–8 August 1844], p. 148 & 151, (23 & 24 June 1844), Joseph Smith Papers.
17 History, 1838–1856, volume F-1 [1 May 1844–8 August 1844], p. 148, Joseph Smith Papers.
18 History, 1838–1856, volume F-1 [1 May 1844–8 August 1844], p. 151, (24 June 1844), Joseph Smith Papers.
19 Appendix 3: Willard Richards, Journal Excerpt, 23–27 June 1844, Document Transcript, Footnotes, Joseph Smith Papers.

> 3 o'clock. The Governor has just agreed to march his army to Nauvoo and I shall come along with him. . . .
>
> I am as ever
>
> Joseph Smith[20]

Two days later, on June 27 at about 8:00 a.m., Joseph penned:

> Dear Emma . . .
>
> There is no danger of any "exterminating order." Should there be a mutiny among the troops . . . remain loyal, and stand for the defense of the state & our rights; There is one principle which is Eternal, it is the duty of all men to protect their lives and the lives of their households whenever [it] requires. and no power has a right to forbid it. should the last extreme arrive, —but I anticipate no such extreme,—but caution is the parent of safety.—
>
> Joseph Smith
>
> P.S. Dear Emma,
>
> I am very much resigned to my lot, knowing I am justified and have done the best that could be done. Give my love to the children and all my Friends, Mr. Brower and all who inquire after me; and as for treason I know that I have not committed any, and they cannot prove one appearance of any thing of the kind, So you need not have any fears that any harm can happen to us on that score. may God bless you all. Amen.
>
> Joseph Smith[21]

A mob loitered outside the Carthage jail, where Joseph and Hyrum were imprisoned, and sang, "Where now is the Prophet Joseph? Where now is the Prophet Joseph? Where now is the Prophet Joseph? Safe in Carthage jail!"[22] Even the governor of Illinois, though not a participant in boisterous song, joined the chorus of conspirators, mobbers, and militia in abetting the deaths of Joseph and Hyrum.

---

20 Letter of Joseph Smith to Emma Smith, June 25, 1844, History, 1838–1856, volume F-1 [1 May 1844–8 August 1844], p. 157, Joseph Smith Papers.

21 Letter of Joseph Smith to Emma Smith, 27 June 1844, pp. 1–[2]. Spelling standardized. Joseph Smith Papers.

22 B. H. Roberts, *A Comprehensive History of The Church of Jesus Christ of Latter-day Saints*. 6 vols. (Provo, UT: Brigham Young University Press, 1965), 2:281.

As the day waned, Joseph, Hyrum, and two members of the Quorum of the Twelve Apostles, John Taylor and Willard Richards, lingered in the east bedroom of the Carthage Jail. There John Taylor was asked to sing "A Poor Wayfaring Man of Grief." The hymn harmonized with the ominous foreboding of near events:

> In pris'n I saw him next, condemned
> To meet a traitor's doom at morn.
> The tide of lying tongues I stemmed,
> And honored him 'mid shame and scorn.
> My friendship's utmost zeal to try.
> He asked if I for him would die.
> The flesh was weak; my blood ran chill,
> But my free spirit cried, "I will!"[23]

Around five in the afternoon of June 27, 1844, Willard Richards saw a hundred or more men running around the corner of the jail. Taylor described them as "an armed mob—painted black—of from 150 to 200 persons" (D&C 135:1). They easily overpowered the jailor, rushed the stairs, and began shooting into the east bedroom. Despite initial attempts to protect themselves from mob violence, the four men were no match for the disguised men.

Hyrum was the first to fall from an assassin's bullet. As he backed away from the door to the center of the room, one bullet pierced the upper panel of the door and struck him on the left side of the nose. As he was falling to the floor, he exclaimed, "*I am a dead man!*" (D&C 135:1). As Joseph moved toward the east bedroom window, two bullets hit him from the doorway, and two struck him from the outside. He fell from the second-story window to the ground below and was heard to exclaim, "*O Lord my God!*" (D&C 135:1). The mob had finished its murderous plot, and Joseph, the Prophet, lay dead outside the jail.

Emma learned of the brutal murder of her husband and his brother Hyrum from her nephew Lorenzo Wasson. Official word was sent soon after daybreak the next day.

> Carthage Jail, 8 o'clock 5 min P. M. June 27th. 1844.
> Joseph and Hyrum are dead. Taylor wounded, not very badly. I am well. Our guard was forced, as we believe, by a band of Missourians from 1 to 200. The job was done in an instant, and the party fled towards Nauvoo instantly. This is as I believe

---

23 "A Poor Wayfaring Man of Grief," *Hymns*, no. 29.

it. The citizens here [Carthage] are afraid of the Mormons attacking them; I promise them *No!*

W[illard] Richards. . . . John Taylor.[24]

Bodies of the Slain Martyrs Return to Nauvoo

About 8:00 a.m. on Friday, June 28, the remains of Joseph and Hyrum were placed in rough boxes, put into two wagons, and then covered with prairie hay, blankets, and bushes to protect them from the hot sun. A guard of eight soldiers led by Samuel H. Smith was detached to escort the remains to Nauvoo. Between 2:30 and 3 p.m., the funeral procession moved along Mulholland Street, where the assembled Nauvoo Legion, city council, and thousands of mourners vented their sorrow. The procession passed by the unfinished temple, where additional crowds had gathered, and then turned down Main Street to the Mansion House. Mary Rich reported, "The people were almost frantic to get one little glimpse of him, but they were driven back by the marshall. The wagon was driven inside the back gate and the gate was locked. No one was allowed in the yard except the guards and the Prophet's special friends."[25]

The eight to ten thousand Saints assembled near the Mansion House heard brief remarks from Church leaders. Most remembered were the words of Willard Richards, who "pledged his honor and his life for their good conduct." The people "with one united voice resolved to trust to the law for a remedy of such a high handed assassination; and when that failed, to call upon God to avenge them of their wrongs." Richards concluded, "O! Americans weep, for the glory of freedom has departed."[26] Those assembled were admonished to go home quietly and promised that beginning at eight o'clock in the morning of June 29, the remains of the martyrs could be viewed by all.

Meanwhile, inside the Manson House, Dimick B. Huntington, William Marks, and William D. Huntington washed the bodies in preparation for the public viewing. Camphor-soaked cotton was placed in each gunshot wound,

---

24 History, 1838–1856, volume F-1 [1 May 1844–8 August 1844], p. 185, (27 June 1844), Joseph Smith Papers.
25 "Life of Mary Ann Rich: 1820–1912," 17, as cited in Susan Easton Black, "The Tomb of Joseph," *The Disciple as Witness: Essays on Latter-day Saint History and Doctrine in Honor of Richard Lloyd Anderson,* Stephen D. Ricks, Donald W. Parry, and Andrew H. Hedges, ed. (Provo, UT: F.A.R.M.S. 2000), p. 1049.
26 History, 1838–1856, volume F-1 [1 May 1844–8 August 1844], p. 188, (28 June 1844), Joseph Smith Papers.

and the bodies were dressed in "fine plain drawers and shirts, white neckerchiefs white cotton stockings and white shrouds."[27]

Widows of the deceased, Emma Smith and Mary Fielding Smith, were among the first to view the bodies. Emma hesitated before saying, "Now I can see him; I am strong now." She then walked toward his casket and "kneeled down, clasped him around his face and sank upon his body. She exclaimed, 'Joseph, Joseph, are you dead? Have the assassins shot you?'"[28] According to Joseph Smith III, Emma cried, "Oh, Joseph Joseph! My husband, my husband! Have they taken you from me at last!"[29]

Lucy Mack Smith wrote of her sorrow:

> I had for a long time braced every nerve, roused every energy of my soul, and called upon God to strengthen me; but when I entered the room, and saw my murdered sons, extended both at once before my eyes; and heard the sobs and groans of my family – the cries of "Father! Husband! Brothers!" from the lips of their wives, children, brother and sisters, it was too much—I sunk back crying to the Lord in the agony of my soul, My God! My God! Why has thou forsaken this family? A voice replied, I have taken them to myself that they might have rest.[30]

On June 29, "thousands came from all quarters to take a last look; and steamboats loaded with strangers came from Burlington, Quincy, and many other places to look upon their dead bodies," reported Sarah Rich. Eliza R. Snow poetically wrote of the grief expressed in the Mansion House and on the streets of Nauvoo:

> All hearts with sorrow bleed, and ev'ry eye
> Is bath'd in tears—each bosom heaves a sigh—
> Heart broken widows' agonizing groans,
> Are mingled with the helpless orphans' moans!

---

27 History, 1838–1856, volume F-1 [1 May 1844–8 August 1844], p. 188, (28 June 1844), Joseph Smith Papers.
28 Newell and Avery, *Mormon Enigma*, p. 197.
29 B. W. Richmond, "The Prophet's Death!" *Deseret Evening News* 9, no. 5 (November 27, 1875): 3, as cited in Newell and Avery, *Mormon Enigma*, p. 197.
30 Lucy Mack Smith, History, 1845, pp. 312–313. Joseph Smith Papers.

> Ye Saints! be still, and know that God is just—
> With steadfast purpose in his promise trust.
> Girded with sackcloth, own his mighty hand,
> And wait his judgements on this guilty land![31]

On June 29 at 5:00 p.m., the Mansion House was cleared of mourners. Coffins containing the remains of Joseph and Hyrum Smith were concealed in a bedroom closet in the northeast corner of the Mansion House. Carefully placed into an awaiting wagon/hearse were rough pine boxes filled with bags of sand in place of the martyrs' remains. As the mock funeral procession began, the cortege moved down Main Street, passed by the temple, and stopped at the burial vault. A "mock burial" was conducted inside the vault located south of the Nauvoo Temple.[32]

About midnight on June 29, coffins containing the bodies of Joseph and Hyrum Smith were taken from the Mansion House and carried through the garden to the Nauvoo House. The bodies were interred in the basement story of the uncompleted structure. The ground was then flattened and covered with chips of wood, stone, and other rubbish to camouflage the site. That evening, a violent rainstorm removed any trace of the real burial site of Joseph and Hyrum Smith.[33]

---

31 Eliza R. Snow, "The Assassination of Gen'ls Joseph Smith and Hyrum Smith, First Presidents of the Church of Latter Day Saints: who were massacred by a Mob, in Carthage, Hancock County, Ill, on the 27th June 1844," *Times and Seasons* 5, no. 12 (July 1, 1844): 575.

32 See Richard Van Wagoner and Steven C. Walker, "The Joseph/Hyrum Smith Funeral Sermon," *BYU Studies* 23, no. 1 (1983): 3–7.

33 See Susan Easton Black, "The Tomb of Joseph," 61–86.

Chapter Seven
WIDOW TO SECOND MARRIAGE

EMMA DID NOT RETREAT INTO the dark recesses of the Mansion House after Joseph's death. She actively tried to clarify her role as a widow. Emma was not left without means. Beginning on May 15, 1841, she had acquired farmland for $2,700 in Hancock County from Ebenezer and Eleanor Wiggins. From that date until June 27, 1844, Emma's name, and that of her children, appeared on multiple land transactions. She and her children owned three parcels of land outside of Nauvoo and twenty-eight parcels in town.

Conflicts between Emma and Church Leadership

Questions arose as to whether the properties in Emma's name and those of her children and properties in the name of Joseph Smith belonged to the family or to The Church of Jesus Christ of Latter-day Saints. For example, Emma held the title to the lot on which the unfinished Nauvoo House stood, but she did not hold the title to the building. The fact that Joseph Smith did not leave a last will and testament and made little distinction between property transactions to provide for his family and property transactions of Church holdings were real, and decisive answers were not easy to come by.

Creditors were not willing to wait for property ownership issues to be resolved by legal means. They wanted to be paid immediately for Joseph's expenditures, and Emma became their prey. Emma expressed her frustrations in a letter to Thomas Gregg: "I have no documents or papers in my possession of a historical character whatever. All the records of Mr. Smith's of that nature were left with Willard Richards and Wm Clayton."[1]

Another issue between Emma and Church leaders was Joseph Smith's translation of the Bible. On August 19, 1844, Willard Richards called on "Emma Smith, widow of the Prophet, for the new translation of the *Bible*: She

---

1 Letter of Emma Smith to Thomas Gregg, April 21, 1846 as quoted in Newell and Avery, *Mormon Enigma*, p. 234.

said she did not feel disposed to give it up at present."[2] However, Emma did allow John Bernhisel to read the new translation manuscript. Bernhisel copied the manuscript markings into his own Bible, which he later gave to Brigham Young and wrote,

> I had great desires to see the new Translation, but did not like to ask for it: but one evening, being at Bro. Joseph's house about a year after his death, Sister Emma to my surprise asked me if I would not like to see it. I answered yes. She handed it to me the next day, and I kept it in my custody about three months. She told me it was not prepared for the press, as Joseph had designed to go through it again. I did not copy all that was translated leaving some few additions and changes that were made in some of the books. But so far as I did copy, I did so as correctly as I could.[3]

Of her possessing Joseph Smith's translation of the Bible, Emma said, "I never had any fear that the house would burn down as long as the Inspired Translation of the Bible was in it. I always felt safe when it was in the house, for I knew it could not be destroyed."[4] Emma retained possession of the new translation until 1867, when she gave the manuscript to her son Joseph Smith III. "If I had trusted all that wished the privilege [to copy them or have them] you would not have had them in your possession now," she said.[5]

Then there was the issue of Emma moving the remains of Joseph and Hyrum Smith in September 1844 without informing Mary Fielding Smith or Brigham Young. The bodies were buried thirty-eight feet south and twenty feet west of the southwest corner of the Homestead under the "bee house."[6] Joseph III recalled seeing the second burial and watching as a lock of hair was cut from his father's

---

2   Smith, *History of the Church*, 7:260.
3   Statement of John Bernhisel, in L. John Nuttall, "Diary One," September 10, 1879, 335, as cited in Robert L. Millet, "Joseph Smith's Translation of the Bible: A Historical Overview," in *The Joseph Smith Translation: The Restoration of Plain and Precious Truths,* Monte S. Nyman and Robert L. Millet, ed. (Provo, UT: Religious Studies Center, Brigham Young University, 1985).
4   Edmund C. Briggs, "A Visit to Nauvoo in 1856," *Journal of History* 9, no. 4 (October 1916): 460.
5   Emma Smith Bidamon to Joseph Smith III, December 2, 1867; Emma Hale Smith Letters, 1866-1871, as cited in Roger D. Launius, *Joseph Smith III: Pragmatic Prophet* (Urbana and Chicago: University of Illinois Press, 1995), p. 39.
6   Black, "The Tomb of Joseph," p. 66.

head and given to his mother. She placed the hair in a locket.7 At the general conference in October 1845, Brigham Young declared,

> We will petition Sister Emma in the name of Israel's God, to let us deposit the remains of Joseph according as he commanded us [in a tomb in Nauvoo]. And if she will not consent to it, our garments are clear.—Then when he wakes in the morning of the resurrection, he shall talk with [her], not with me; the sin shall be upon her head—not ours."8

The remains of Joseph and Hyrum Smith were never laid in the tomb prepared for them in Nauvoo.

Birth of David Hyrum Smith

On November 17, 1844, Emma gave birth to David Hyrum Smith in the Mansion House. "Emma gave birth to a son," Mrs. Durfee said, claiming "Joseph the prophet" had named the baby before he left for Carthage. According to Mrs. Durfee, the baby was born "to be the David the Bible speaks of to rule over Israel forever."9

Eliza R. Snow composed a poem commemorating the birth of David Hyrum Smith. A few stanzas read:

> Sinless as celestial spirits—
> Lovely as a morning flow'r,
> Comes the smiling infant stranger
> In an evil-omen'd hour.
>
> In an hour of lamentation—
> In a time—a season when
> Zion's noblest sons are fallen,
> By the hands of wicked men. . . .
>
> Not to share a father's fondness—
> Not to know a father's worth—
> By the arm of persecution
> 'Tis an orphan at its birth!
> Smile, sweet babe! thou art unconscious

---

7 Joseph Smith III, *Joseph Smith III and the Restoration* Mary Audentia Smith Anderson, ed. (Independence, MO: Herald House, 1952), p. 85.
8 "General Conference," *Millennial Star* 7, no. 2 (January 15, 1846), pp. 23–24.
9 Oliver Huntington Journal, p. 53, as cited in Newell and Avery, *Mormon Enigma*, p. 211.

Of thy great, untimely loss!
The broad stroke of thy bereavement,
Zion's pathway seem'd to cross! . . .

Thou may'st draw from love and kindness
All a mother can bestow;
But alas! on earth, a father
Thou art destin'd not to know![10]

The *New York Sun*

The *New York Sun* of December 9, 1845, printed a letter allegedly written by Emma on November 20, 1845, just days after giving birth to David Hyrum Smith. The letter reads,

> This church, such as it is, was formed by my lamented husband who was martyred for its sake, and whether true or false, has laid down his life for its belief! I am left here, sir, with a family of children to attend to, without any means of giving them an education, *for there is not a school in the city*, nor is it intended there shall be any here, or at any other place, where the men who now govern this infatuated, simple-minded people, have sway. I have not the least objection that the petty tyrants remove to California, or at any other remote place, out of the world if they wish; for they will never be of any service to the Mormons, or the human family, no matter where they go.
>
> *I must now say, that I have never for a moment believed in what my husband called his apparitions and revelations, as I thought him laboring under a diseased mind*; yet they may all be true, as a Prophet is seldom without credence or honor, excepting in his own family or country . . .
>
> With great respect,
> I am, sir, your humble serv't
> Emma Smith[11]

Eleven days after the letter appeared in the *Sun*, Emma wrote to James Arlington Bennett, editor of the *New York Sun*. "I never was more confounded with a misrepresentation than I am with that letter, and I am greatly perplexed

---

10 Eliza R. Snow, "Lines written on the birth of an infant son of Mrs. Emma, widow of the late General Joseph Smith," *Times and Seasons* 5, no. 22 (December 1, 1844): 735.
11 As cited in Newell and Avery, *Mormon Enigma*, pp. 222–223.

that *you* should entertain the *impression* that the document should be a genuine production of mine. How could you believe me capable of so much treachery?"12

Emma asked that the following letter be printed in the *Sun*:

> I wish to inform you, and the public through your paper, that the letter published Tuesday morning, December 9th, is a forgery, the whole of it, and I hope that this notice will put a stop to all such communications.
> Emma Smith.

Emma's letter was never printed in the *Sun* but did appear in the *Times and Seasons* on January 15, 1846, with this assurance—

> [Emma] honored her husband while living, and she will never knowingly dishonor his good name while his martyred blood mingles with mother earth! Mrs. Smith is an honorable woman . . . The very idea that so valuable and beloved a lady, could be coaxed into a fame of *disgrace* . . . is as cruel and bloody as the assassination of her husband at Carthage.
> The fact is, the story must have been put in circulation to injure the Latter Day Saints; and as Mrs. Smith was one of them, to destroy or murder her reputation, and create division in the church.13

Would Emma Join the Mormon Exodus?

After the birth of David Hyrum Smith, Emma was not seen rushing about Nauvoo like most in town. She was certainly aware that thousands of Latter-day Saints were moving about in what presented a most unusual dichotomy—an oddity of grand proportions. With dogged determination, they worked to complete the temple, their homes, and their shops and to cultivate their farms. Yet those who built the city also scurried to build wagons to transport themselves and their families to regions unknown and uncharted in the Rocky Mountains.

As Latter-day Saints made their final preparations to leave Nauvoo, several tried to second-guess the future plans of Emma as to whether she would follow Brigham Young to the west or remain in Nauvoo. Believing that she would stay in Nauvoo, a few of the Saints gave Emma their properties for "$1 and love

---

12 Letter of Emma Smith to General James Arlington Bennet, as cited in Newell and Avery, *Mormon Enigma*, p. 224.
13 Newell and Avery, *Mormon Enigma*, p. 213.

and consideration." Other Saints paid Emma a visit at the Mansion House to bid her farewell. Wilford Woodruff called on Emma and expressed concern for her well-being and safety. Emma gave Wilford a cane created from the oak box that carried Joseph's body from Carthage to the Mansion House and a pair of white cotton gloves. To his wife, Phoebe, she gave a handkerchief. Other Latter-day Saints wrote letters expressing their love for her.

> Dear Sister Emma,
> I cannot take my departure from this place, without acknowledging the debt of gratitude that I am under to you. And in making this acknowledgement, I especially desire to be understood that I am observing no more form or idle custom, nor empty ceremony. During the three years that I was a member of your family, I found every necessary provided for my comfort, with much order and neatness, and from yourself and family I experienced not only kindness and respect, but such affectionate regard, tenderness and delicacy as to make me feel more than your grateful friend—I may never be permitted to pay you all; but the bond of obligation shall ever remain binding on my heart and life. And I beg you to accept my profound and grateful acknowledgements for your uniform kindness and attention to me, and for your trouble of me during so long a period; and I fervently pray that God may reward you in this world a thousand-fold and in the world to come with life everlasting.
> —J. M. Bernhisel[14]

Fulton City, Illinois

Emma's immediate concern was for her own safety and that of her children. In the September 1846 Battle of Nauvoo, Emma was threatened that "if she did not move out of the house in three days, it would be burned over her head."[15] On the third day of the battle, Emma discovered a pile of charred sticks and leaves had been placed against the north side of her house. Fearing that arsonists would burn her house to the ground, Emma placed care of the Mansion House in the hands of Abram Van Tuyl and boarded the steamer *Uncle Toby* with her children and housekeeper, Savilla Durfee. After a six-day voyage with Captain

---

14 John M. Bernhisel to Emma Smith, October 9, 1847, John Milton Bernhisel Collection, 1829-1894, John Milton Bernhisel, Papers 1818–1872, as cited in Newell and Avery, *Mormon Enigma*, p. 245.

15 Smith, *Joseph Smith III and the Restoration*, p. 88.

Grimes at the helm, Emma and her family disembarked at Fulton City, about 150 miles upstream from Nauvoo.

In Fulton, Emma rented a large two-story frame house at the corner of Base and Wall Streets. She and her family shared rooms with friends who had also fled from Nauvoo. One friend wrote,

> [Emma] won respect and esteem for herself despite the prejudice many felt against the name "Mormon." I had more than a casual acquaintance with her, and knew her to be a rare good woman . . . a devoted mother. It seems to me that the rocky hills of Pennsylvania had developed in her a character of uprightness and integrity that carried her bravely through trials that would have overwhelmed women of [a] more common mould.[16]

Emma and her children resided in Fulton City from September 1846 until February 1847. Of their residency, Joseph III recalled, "My sister Julia and I were well received in to the younger social circles of that little town. A love for social functions was awakened at that time within me and from the date of our return to Nauvoo, I mingled freely in the society of the place."[17]

The reason Emma returned with her family to Nauvoo was news of Abram Van Tuyl having built a houseboat and intending to furnish his boat with furniture from the Mansion House. Any furniture he didn't use in the houseboat was to be sold downriver as Van Tuyl was on his way to Texas. Hoping to stop his shenanigans, Emma returned to Nauvoo. Her grandson Elbert A. Smith wrote in verse:

> [At] Fulton City – [Grandmother Smith explained,]
> "I made up my mind
> I had no friend
> left but God &
> no place to go
> but home."[18]

Emma Returns to Nauvoo

Grandson Elbert Aorial Smith said, "[Emma] reached Nauvoo in the afternoon of February 19, 1847, and so determinedly pushed her claims, that

---

16 Fulton (Ill.) Journal, May 30, 1879, as cited in Newell and Avery, *Mormon Enigma*, p. 240.
17 Joseph Smith III, *The Memoirs of President Joseph Smith III (1832–1914): A Photo-Reprint Edition of the Original Serial Publication as Edited by Mary Audentia Smith Anderson and appearing in the Saints' Herald* (November 6, 1934–July 31, 1937). Richard P. Howard, ed. (Independence, MO: Herald House, 1979), p. 80; S. Reed Murdock, *Joseph and Emma's Julia, The "Other Twin"* (Salt Lake City: Eborn Books, 2004), p. 80.
18 Elbert Aoriul Smith Reminiscences, as quoted in Youngreen, *Reflections of Emma*, p. 129.

in three days she was again installed in her house as its mistress."[19] The Nauvoo Emma returned to was much different from the Nauvoo she had left. Like Thomas L. Kane, Emma found "empty workshops, ropewalks, and smithies."[20] Like Charles Lanman, Emma discovered "of the houses left standing, not more than one out of ten was occupied . . . hardly a window retained a full pane of glass, and the doors were broken, and open, and hingeless."[21] Joseph Smith III wrote an even more disparaging description of Nauvoo:

> From 1846 to as late as 1855, Nauvoo which once enjoyed a good reputation, was a place of disgrace and disorder. Saloons were many and ran wide open, proprietors and patrons alike being shiftless, thieving, drinking boisterous and thoroughly unprofitable citizens. Among the boarders at our hotel could be found men of all classes. Considerable transient traffic moved to and fro up and down the river, and the Mansion drew its share of this sort of public patronage. In the winter season we usually had, in addition to regular borders, numbers of such patrons whom we termed "river men."[22]

Lewis Crum Bidamon

Lewis Crum Bidamon, the son of Dedrich "John" Bidamon and Mary Crum, was born in 1802 in western Virginia. About 1824 Lewis married Nancy Sebree of Pickaway County, Iowa. To their union were born three children. By 1832, Lewis and Nancy were residing in the small town of Canton, Illinois. There Lewis constructed a house on the Canton public square and helped establish the first Congregational Church. He purchased the Ellis Steam Mill in Canton and converted it into a carriage factory. After the death of his wife, Nancy, Lewis married Mary Ann Douglas, a widow in 1842. Four months later, their marriage ended.

Joseph Smith had a business relationship with Lewis Bidamon and his brothers. Joseph ordered carriages from Lewis and hired his brother John Bidamon to run the Red Brick Store. Their brother, Christian Bidamon, rented rooms in the Mansion House.

---

19   Inez A. Kennedy, *Recollections of the Pioneers of Lee County, Illinois, 1893*, Ronald E. Romig, ed. *Emma's Family* (Independence, MO: John Whitmer Books, 2008), p. 11.
20   Thomas L. Kane quote, in E. Cecil McGavin, *The Nauvoo Temple* (Salt Lake City: Deseret Book, 1962), p. 122.
21   Statement of Charles Lanman, quoted in E. Cecil McGavin, *The Nauvoo Temple* (Salt Lake City: Deseret Book, 1962), p. 121.
22   Murdock, *Joseph and Emma's Julia*, p. 80.

When raids on Latter-day Saint farms led to the destruction of property and threats to property owners, Lewis Bidamon was given direct orders by Governor Thomas Ford to deliver instructions to the state militia commander to control the mobs, recruit a force, and proceed to Nauvoo.[23] More important to the relationship of Lewis and Emma, however, is a business letter.

> Canton Fulton Co Ills
> January 11th 1847
> Dear Madam
> I Wright to you from this place where I have beenn ever Since our defeat at Nauvoo I was taken sick shortly after I arrived here with the Bilious Fever almost despaired of recovery by my physician and Friends My recovery is very Slow I am only now able to walk about the House My Brother John and Family have moved back and I Shall return as soon as my health will admit of Traveling They tell me there is nothing but peace and tranquility there existing . . .
> My Brother John and myself are desirous to Rent the Mansion House of you if you intend letting it and if So please inform me what will be your Terms per annum we wish to Rent House, Barn, and Furniture, in fine everything that pertains to the Tavern Pleas excuse this bill. I am very nervous.
> Your Sincere Friend and well Wisher
> —Lewis Bidamon[24]

Emma replied to the inquiry—

> January 1847
> Mr Bidamon
> Yours of the 11th January came to [me] was received yesterday, in answer to which I have to say, that I suppose I shall have to get possession of the Mansion before I can rent it again, as I do not expect You would like to rent it and run the risk of getting possession as I do not know as Dr. Van T will be willing to give up the property he has in his possession indeed

---

23 "Biography of Lewis Crum Bidamon"; Based on Edward A. Luce, "The Bidamon Story," MS 7459, f2, items 5, 6, LDS Church History Library.
24 Letter of Lewis Bidamon to Emma Smith, January 11, 1847. Spelling standardized. Emma Smith Papers, P4, f28, Community of Christ Archives, as cited in Romig, *Emma's Family,* p. 15.

> I do expect Some trouble with him yet before I get out of [it] . . . I want to rent the farm that is near Na[uvoo]. If you know of someone that wishes to rent it you would do me a favour to let me know of it. Upland I have another farm between the Quincy road and Warsaw near the Marshes that I wish to rent or sell I also have a number of City lots in Nauvoo I would like to sell. I am anxiously waiting to know what our new Governor is a going to do with regard to the affairs of Hancock.
>
> I formed a very agreeable acquaintance with your brothers Fr. [Frederick's] family while on the boat with them and would be pleased to see them again and that too under more pleasant circumstances. You will please give them my best respects
>
> Yours Truly, [Emma Smith][25]

By summer of 1847, Lewis had moved to Nauvoo and was a storekeeper. By fall of 1847, he was courting Emma. Joseph III remembered Lewis calling upon his mother—

> Catching sight of Mother sewing at an upper window, he made her a very polite and widely sweeping bow. Regaining his erect posture after this elaborate ceremony, he replaced his hat upon his head and stepped forward briskly, when suddenly a clothesline he had failed to observe caught him across the forehead, just under the brim of his hat! Off flew the hat, but alas, along with it flew a very fine toupee.[26]

Emma laughed as Lewis shouted, "Damn that wig!" According to Joseph III, "[The] embarrassing situation . . . proved no handicap to the gallant gentleman, for he was made of sterner stuff."[27]

Lewis and Emma were married on Thursday, December 23, 1847—the very day in December that Joseph Smith was born in Sharon, Vermont, forty-two years before—by Reverend William Hany, a Methodist minister in Nauvoo. Due to a Methodist minister officiating at her wedding, questions arose about whether Emma had joined the Methodist faith. She set the question to rest by

---

25 Letter of Emma Smith to Lewis Bidamon, January 1847. Spelling standardized. Emma Smith Papers, P4, f28, Community of Christ Archives; Romig, as cited in Romig, *Emma's Family*, p. 15.
26 Smith, *Joseph Smith and the Restoration*, pp. 94–95, as cited in Newell and Avery, *Mormon Enigma*, p. 246.
27 Smith, *Joseph Smith and the Restoration*, p. 95, as cited in Newell and Avery, *Mormon Enigma*, p. 246.

saying, "I have been called apostate; but I have never apostatized, nor forsaken the faith I at first accepted."[28]

Sarah M. Kimball wrote to Nancy Marinda Hyde about the wedding of Lewis and Emma:

> The marriage of Mrs. Smith is the all-absorbing topic of conversation. She was married last Thursday eve, the groom, Mr. Bidamon, is, I believe, looked upon with universal contempt. He was a widower, wears a wig, has two daughters, young ladies. A Mrs. Kinney, who credits him with one child, says he still loves her, but married Emy [Emma] for her property. Mrs. Smith manifested the confidence she has in her intended husband by employing attorneys to execute a marriage contract and secure to her all the Property. The ceremony was performed by Rev. Methodist Mr. Hany. The bride was dressed in plum colored satin, a lace tuck handkerchief, gold watch and chain, no cap, hair plain. . . . We were not honored guests but we were told that things passed off very genteelly.[29]

News of the marriage was reported to Brigham Young by John Fullmer: "I suppose you know by this time that there was a certain widow in this place, who was lately given (and as the orthodoxy would say) 'in holy matrimony' to one of his Satanic Majesty's high priests, to wit, one Lewis Bidamon."[30] Although Fullmer saw the marriage of Emma and Lewis as inappropriate, others did not, including Emma and her children.

---

28 Smith, "Last Testimony of Sister Emma," *Saints' Herald* 26, no. 19 (October 1, 1879): 290, col. 1.
29 Letter of Sarah M. Kimball to Nancy Marinda Hyde, January 2, 1848. Church History Library.
30 Letter of John Fullmer to Brigham Young, January 26, 1848, in Crawford Notes, as quoted in Newell and Avery, *Mormon Enigma*, p. 247.

Chapter Eight
CHOICES

An advertisement in the *Valley Whig & Keokuk Registry* announced "commodious and well-known Hotel [the Mansion House] has recently undergone a thorough repair, and with new furniture, etc." The advertisement boasted of accommodations being "in a superior style" and of Nauvoo being a "healthy or pleasant location in the Mississippi valley to spend the summer months, it being a fine situation of country for hunting, and the river at this place abounds with the finest of fish. One of the largest and best arranged Stables in the Western country is connected with the House."[1] The notice also reflected a change in Emma's life:

> In 1848, JULIA MARRIED
> Elisha Dixon who took over
> management of the Mansion.
> Nauvoo Mansion
> Main Street, Nauvoo, Illinois.[2]

Due to poor health, Elisha Dixon relinquished management of the hotel. Emma, once again, took over as manager. She was not only expected to welcome and accommodate customers, but she also had the burden of running a hotel that was financially insolvent. She attributed her financial woes to the burning of the Nauvoo Temple. On October 9, 1848, the temple was severely damaged by an unidentified incendiary. Fire reduced the magnificent temple to an eyesore, a blackened shell of limestone. Paying guests at the Mansion House dropped by a fourth when the temple burned.

---

1 *Valley Whig & Keokuk Registry*, June 21, 1849, as cited in Romig, *Emma's Family*, p. 28.
2 *Valley Whig & Keokuk Registry*, June 21, 1849, as cited in Romig, *Emma's Family*, p. 28.

The Gold Fields of California

With finances spiraling ever downward, news of a gold rush in California was welcomed. Lewis and his brother John made plans to join gold seekers traveling overland to California in 1849. After only eighteen months of marriage, Lewis left Emma to pan for gold. He and his brother crossed the Mississippi in late April 1849 and joined a wagon train of "Forty-Niners" heading to California.

On May 4, Lewis wrote to Emma, "Our journey so far is very pleasant . . . I have nothing to regret in determining the undertaking this jaunt only being separated from her—that I *love* and the Society of the Children." In his letter, Lewis revealed a sense of humor. He told of a cooked squirrel being placed on a table and of the table being accidentally knocked over. His brother John reached down to grasp the squirrel meat. "Thinking he had found a piece and applying it to his tasters to his great astonishment found it to be not buffalo chip but Cow chip. Didn't he Spit! Good by for the present Your dear Husband LC Bidamon."[3]

In a May 21, 1849, letter written in Kanesville, Iowa, Lewis informed Emma, "The Mormons receive us very kindly and appear to feel a deep entrust in your welfare . . . The gold news is Still increasing and more flattering the farther west we get." He closed the letter with words of affection: "O Emma that I could even have the privilege of your Society as long as I am penning these reflections I would hold it priceless. I remain your affectionate Husband until death L C Bidamon."[4]

On July 5, 1849, Lewis wrote of being in Indian Territory "after a tedious travel over the black hills or rather barren mountains and once burning volcanoes we past for miles over earth and stones." He again closed his letter to Emma with affection.

> O my love if I could only hear from you and know that you was . . . enjoying yourselves it would ease this acking heart it would over compare with the brilliant prospects of my Success in California Be cheerful Dear, if we live the day will arrive when we will meet again and press each other to our congenios breasts fare you well for the present
> L. C. Bidamon[5]

---

3   Letter of Lewis Crum Bidamon to Emma Smith Bidamon, May 4, 1849, as cited in Newel and Avery, *Mormon Enigma*, p. 252. Spelling standardized.
4   Letter of Lewis C. Bidamon to Emma Smith Bidamon, May 21, 1849. Spelling standardized. Miscellaneous Collection, P87, f5, Community of Christ Archives, as cited in Romig, *Emma's Family*, pp. 20–21.
5   Letter of Lewis Crum Bidamon to Emma Smith Bidamon, July 5, 1849. Spelling standardized. Lewis C. Bidamon Papers, P12-2, f13, Community of Christ Archives, as cited in Romig, *Emma's Family*, pp. 22–23.

On August 16, from Cross Creek, California, Lewis estimated that he and his brother John were "16 hundred . . . miles from _N[auvoo]." He told Emma their "prospect for getting to the gold regions _[looks] more favorable . . . we are all well and in good spirits . . . Suffice it to say we have past through the [valley] of death I will return as soon as I _[can]_ and then will take pleasure in ac[counting] our whole trip – L. C. Bidamon."6

As Lewis was having one adventure after another, Emma had few. She was forced to sell properties to pay taxes at a time when property values in Nauvoo had plummeted. Furthermore, a John Bernhisel letter of September 10, 1849, described forty-five-year-old Emma as having become "quite corpulent."7

The only extant letter of Emma to Lewis was written on January 7, 1850—

> My dear Lewis,
> I have scarcely enjoyed any good thing since you left home, in consequence of the terrifying apprehension that you might be suffering for the most common comfort of life. I have never been weary without thinking that you might be much more so. I never have felt the want of food without fear that you might be almost or quite starving and I have never [been] thirsty without feeling my heart quicken with the reflection that perhaps you were sinking, faint and famished for want of that reviving draught.

She then told Lewis of her financial crisis—

> I have been trying to Save some property but I can assure you that my Chance of saving property is just as good as a woman's Chance would be in the fifth Story of a burning building in Broad Way N.Y. when You might see her standing in the front window holding her most precious goods in her hands, hesitating whether to throw her goods back into the flames, or throw them into the streets among the thieves.

News of financial reverses were followed by her negative impression of Utah Mormons—

---

6   Letter of Lewis Crum Bidamon to Emma Smith Bidamon, August 16, 1849. Spelling standardized. Lewis C. Bidamon Papers, P12-2, f13, Community of Church Archives, as cited in Romig, *Emma's Family,* p. 24.

7   Letter of John M. Bernhisel to Brigham Young, September 10, 1849, as cited in Valeen Tippetts Avery, *From Mission to Madness: Last Son of the Mormon Prophet* (Urban and Chicago: University of Illinois Press, 1998), p. 34. Spelling standardized.

> My dear Lewis You cannot realize how thankful I was when I learned that You had got from the Bluffs safe and did not go by the valley. I want you should be particularly Cautious of those Mormons for I believe they intend that I shall not enjoy anything without trial. Perhaps you do not need any Caution from me. You might have seen enough to convince you that their intentions are anything but good, yet I must say again keep a good wash [watch] towards them, it may seem strange and ungrateful to You that they should even wish you harmed, and so it is, but I can tell you they are Capable of as infamous ingratitude as any other beings. All that I Can find that they have against You is they think that you occupy a Situation here that you have no business.

Emma concluded her lengthy letter by asking, "O! when Can I begin to think about your Coming home."[8]

On April 20, 1850, Lewis wrote his last letter to Emma from California—

> Gold is not as easy obtained nor in such abundance in California as was and is anticipated by the people of the States it is obtained by the hardest of labour, harder than my constitution is able to bare . . . I do not like California it affords no charms for me and especially in the absence of her and only her that can make me happy . . . Adieu, Dear Emma, for the present. Give my warmest affections to the children and all inquiring friends, and curses to my enemies.[9]

Lewis returned to Nauvoo in 1850, having traveled through the Panama Canal and up the Mississippi River. Whatever gold he may or may not have found was gone by the time he reached Nauvoo.

Lucy Mack Smith

Being in very precarious circumstances, income from hotel guests, especially long-term guests, was all-important. In 1851, Lucy Mack Smith moved into the Mansion House as a long-term guest. In the years that followed, Lucy spent much time in bed and in a wheelchair built by Lewis Bidamon. She suffered

---

8   Letter of Emma Smith Bidamon to Lewis C. Bidamon, January 7, 1850, pp. 26–30, as cited in Romig, *Emma's Family*, pp. 26-30. Spelling standardized.

9   Letter of Lewis C. Bidamon to Emma Smith Bidamon, April 20, 1850, Lewis C. Bidamon Papers, P12-oo2, f14, Community of Christ Archives, as cited in Romig, *Emma's Family*, pp. 32–33. Spelling standardized.

from rheumatism, which caused her feet, hands, and arms to be distorted and misshapen.

By 1855, Lucy was living in the Joseph Smith farmhouse, a few miles southeast of town. There she resided with Joseph III and his bride, Emeline Griswold. On July 2, 1855, John Lyman Smith reported, "Aunt Lucy has been confined to the bed for ten months unable to walk with the rheumatism."[10] In November 1855, Enoch Tripp wrote that Lucy was "living in a lonely room in the eastern part of the house."[11] Lucy died on May 14, 1856, at age eighty-one. Joseph III wrote to John Bernhisel: "Grandmother died the morning of the 14th of May last easily and with her senses to the last moment. . . . I sat by her and held her hand in mine till death relieved her—The first death scene I ever witnessed."[12] The next day, May 15, 1856, Lucy was buried in the Smith cemetery near the Joseph Smith Homestead in Nauvoo.

Daily Life

Other than the residency and death of Lucy Smith, the 1850s are viewed as the silent decade of Emma's life. To learn of her whereabouts and daily activities, the best source is her grandchildren Emma Smith McCallum and Frederick Alexander Smith. An interview with granddaughter Emma Smith McCallum reveals snippets of Emma's daily life:

> [Grandmother] kept cows, made own
> butter "Dutch" cheese
> wooden churn & dasher
> Dairy house in old horse barn
> Had in time when ran hotel . . .
>   Knitt[in]g lying on a table
> all time – sit to read
> she'd Knit
> Necessities in house
> but no luxuries or
> handsome furnishing. . . .
>   Later years did all
> her own work. Washing &
> all no machine. . . .

---

10 John Lyman Smith Journal, July 2, 1855. Church History Library.
11 Enoch B. Tripp Journal, November 25, 1855, as quoted in Ronald E. Romig, *Lucy's Nauvoo* (Independence, MO: John Whitmer Books, 2009), p. 110.
12 Letter of Joseph Smith III to John Bernhisel, as quoted in Lavina Fielding Anderson, *Lucy's Book: Critical Edition of Lucy Mack Smith's Family Memoirs* (Salt Lake City: Signature Book, 2001), p. 796.

> Everything grew for her;
> pot[atoes], onions, turnips
> cabbage – [She] put in cellar
> grapes—pick & she would
> put wax on end of
> bunch—hang in cellar
> in cool place have
> grapes nearly all winter. . . .
>   [In the] fall have whole string
> of dif[ferent] herbs tied up
> to dry & cure. Made a
> salve – Everybody knew
> of Mother Bidamon's salves[13]

An interview with grandson Frederick Alexander Smith reveals additional glimpses into Emma's daily life:

> Substantial cooking
> pastries – pies
> cookies, doughnuts
> old urn for
> doughnuts
> chickens . . .
>   [She] enjoyed cooking
> but often retired to
> own room to be quiet
> & alone in p.m.[14]

Perhaps more interesting than day-to-day snippets are the insights of grandchildren Emma Smith McCallum and Frederick Alexander Smith into Emma's personality, longings, and sorrows:

> Not given to slang –
> very particular in
> her speech – good
> construction. . . .

---

13 Notebook of Interviews. Emma Smith McCallum's Reminiscences, in Youngreen, *Reflections of Emma*, pp. 55–75. For the complete interview notes, see Mary Audentia Smith Anderson, *Ancestry and Posterity of Joseph Smith and Emma Hale* (Independence, MO: Herald Publishing House, 1939).

14 Notebook of Interviews. Emma Smith McCallum's Reminiscences and Frederick Alexander Smith's Reminiscences, in Youngreen, *Reflections of Emma*, pp. 95, 97.

[Grandmother] loved the River [and] Nauvoo . . .
Deeply religious -believed in B[ook] of M[ormon] – very loyal to church.
Maj. Belonged to no church but he defended her & her church . . .
[Grandmother] loved music – [she] sang – had melodeon [Grandmother would] sing hymns – every ev[enin]g – not [need to] light lamp – [to] sing [because she knew words] by heart
Affectionate in her way but not demonstrative – [Her] aff[ection] was deep – but she manifested it quietly – in service
[Grandmother] could say sharp things – but usually mild-spoken
Heard her speak to tourist – who Somebody tried to Quiz her about why She m[arried]. Maj. Bidamon – her [reply was, "That is a] private affair." . . .
[Grandmother was] healthy all life not quick [of] motion but [could] get around & do more work in a day than most[15]

---

15 Notebook of Interviews. Frederick Alexander Smith's Reminiscences, in Youngreen, *Reflections of Emma*, pp. 57, 93, 95, 97, 101, 105. For the complete interview notes, see Mary Audentia Smith Anderson, *Ancestry and Posterity of Joseph Smith and Emma Hale* (Independence, MO: Herald Publishing House 1929).

Reorganization

Religious confusion permeated the infrastructure of the Church following the martyrdom of the Prophet Joseph Smith. The question of whose right it was to succeed Joseph was asked by Saints, sinners, and fence-sitters. Honest men and women conflicted over the proper course to follow. Designing men with self-aggrandized agendas took advantage of the confused "to lift themselves into positions of authority."[16]

The "Lo, Here!" and "Lo, there!" of the 1840s were reminiscent of an earlier day in Palmyra when young Joseph had wondered, "What is to be done? Who of all these parties are right; or, are they all wrong together?" (JS–History 1:10). Similarly, his devoted followers questioned, "If any one of them be right, which is it, and how shall I know it?" (JS–History 1:10). The struggle to discover light and truth in discordant cries left many disappointed and disillusioned.

Latter-day Saints maintain that the unanimous vote supporting the Quorum of the Twelve Apostles on August 8, 1844, provided the resolution to the religious controversy of succession. Not all of the early Saints would concur. Sidney Rigdon, William Smith, Lyman Wight, and James Strang declared themselves in opposition to the Twelve. They touted their wares, adorned with deceiving glitter, and attracted disciples from among the Saints that had known the Prophet Joseph Smith.

The once-tranquil society of beautiful Nauvoo was in turmoil as Saints were quickly scattered by winds of doctrine in 1845. Hundreds of disillusioned residents left Nauvoo, struggling with religious discord but hoping for harmony. As former citizens fled to Wisconsin, Kentucky, Pennsylvania, and Texas, the strength of cohesive worship dwindled. Listed among those caught in the web of multiple deceptions were Jason W. Briggs and Zenos Gurley, the fathers of the Reorganization movement. By 1851, they had left the main body of Latter-day Saints and were advocating that leadership of the Church belonged to Joseph's oldest son.

Joseph III wrote a detailed account of events leading to his presidency of the Reorganization. In the summer of 1853, he claimed to have his "first serious impressions concerning my connection with the work of my father."[17] He also claimed to see a vision:

> I saw stretched out before me towns, cities, busy marts, courthouses, courts, and assemblies of men, all busy and all

---

16 *The History of the Reorganized Church of Jesus Christ of Latter Day Saints* 8 vols. (Independence, MO: Herald House, 1976), 3:2.

17 *History of the Reorganized Church*, 3:254.

marked by those characteristics that are found in the world, where men win place and renown.... In the subtle transition of a dream I was gazing over a wide expanse of country in a prairie land ... [F]arm and farmhouses, pleasant cot and homelike place, everywhere betokening thrift, industry, and the pursuits of a happy peace were open to the view. I remarked to him standing by me, but whose presence I had not before noticed. "This must be the country of a happy people." To this he replied, "Which would you prefer, life, success, and renown among the busy scenes that you first saw, or a place among these people, without honors or renown? Think of it well, for the choice will be offered to you sooner or later, and you must be prepared to decide. Your decision once made you cannot recall it, and must abide the result."[18]

Joseph III declared he was "at length prepared to answer when the opportunity for the choice should be given."[19] In a letter written to William Marks, he penned, "I am soon going to take my father's place at the head of the Mormon Church, and I wish that you, and some others, those you may consider the most trustworthy, the nearest to you, to come and see; that is, if you can and will."[20] William Marks and others responded by visiting Joseph III in Nauvoo. Rumors of their meeting and of Joseph III's desire to take his father's place were heralded in small Reorganization branches in Wisconsin, Illinois, and Iowa, but surely not among the Latter-day Saints in the West.

There were 150 people at the Reorganization general conference held on April 6, 1860, at 10:00 a.m. in the Mechanics' Hall in Amboy, Illinois. When Joseph III entered the conference with his mother, Emma, by his side, "a strange thrill pervaded the air."[21] After being introduced, Joseph III declared:

I came not here of myself, but by the influence of the Spirit. For some time past I have received manifestations pointing to the position which I am about to assume. I wish to say that I have come here not to be dictated by any men or set of men. I have come in obedience to a power not my own and shall be dictated by that power that sent me.[22]

---

18   *History of the Reorganized Church*, 3:254–255.
19   *History of the Reorganized Church*, 3:255.
20   Letter to William Marks from Joseph Smith III, March 1, 1860, as cited in *History of the Reorganized Church*, 3:264.
21   *History of the Reorganized Church*, 3:265.
22   *History of the Reorganized Church*, 3:247.

On the motion of Isaac Sheen, it was "resolved, that Brother Joseph Smith be chosen Prophet, seer, and Revelator of the Church of Jesus Christ, and the successor of his father."[23] The unanimous vote was followed by a second vote that Emma Bidamon, the fifty-six-year-old widow of the Prophet Joseph and wife of Lewis Bidamon, be received into fellowship. The vote was unanimous in the affirmative.

As a member of the Reorganized Church of Jesus Christ of Latter Day Saints, Emma attended the Olive Branch in Nauvoo. Her grandson Frederick Alexander Smith recalled—

> People came & talked about
> religion—she insisted
> grf [father Joseph Smith] design Joseph [Smith, III] as successor. . . .
>   —used to hold the
> branch prayer meeting
> in her big dining room
> sing &c. —chairs
> Real meeting house upstairs
> In [Grandfather Smith's] brick store—[24]

At the semiannual conference of the Reorganization in October 1860, Emma was appointed to make a selection of hymns and to work with a committee on a hymnbook. The extent of Emma's contribution to the hymnal is unknown. When the hymnbook was printed in Cincinnati, her name did not appear.

---

23 *History of the Reorganized Church*, 3:250.
24 Notebook of Interviews. Frederick Alexander Smith's Reminiscences, in Youngreen, *Reflections of Emma*, pp. 97, 105.

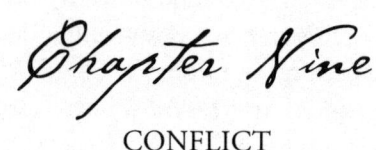

CONFLICT

It was not until 1864 that Emma was confronted with Lewis's infidelity. At age sixty-two, Lewis had an illicit relationship with Nancy Abercrombie, a woman twenty-four years younger than Emma. On March 16, 1864, Nancy gave birth to the illegitimate son of Lewis Bidamon, Charles "Charlie" Edward Bidamon.

Nancy and young Charlie lived by themselves in Nauvoo for four years before moving into the Mansion House—the house in which Emma lived. For some, the mere thought of moving Nancy and Charlie into their home would be repugnant. For Emma, her feelings were not revealed. However, a neighbor wrote of this singular compassionate gesture:

> Mrs. Smith Bidamon was awfully nice. There wasn't a better woman in Nauvoo. She was a good soul, a good christian woman. She was good to everyone. Everyone thought well of her. She was always busy, a great woman to work. She did a good job raising her children. Her boys, Joseph, Alexander, and David were good boys. She was good to Mr. Bidamon's son, Charles.[1]

Letters of Emma to Joseph Smith III

As Emma's children married and had children of their own, they moved on. Although Emma had a crowded household most days, her sons and daughter, Julia, were elsewhere. Emma kept in touch with them through letters. They occasionally came back to the Mansion House for a visit, sometimes for extended periods. Emma was not prone to visit them.

Correspondence with Joseph III reveals her love and admiration for him and her animosity toward Utah Mormons. On February 2–3, 1866, Emma

---

1 Statement of Joseph S. Jemison, August 29, 1940, as quoted in Newell and Avery, *Mormon Enigma*, p. 276.

wrote to Joseph III, "If there is any thing in this world that I am, or ever was proud of it is the honor and integrity of my children but I dare not allow myself to be proud."[2] On August 19, 1866, she wrote again to Joseph III. "Now you must not let those LDSes trouble you too much if they are determined to do evil they will do it and such as are anxiously willing to make you trouble are not worth laboring very hard to save from the dogs."[3]

When her sons Alexander and David Smith accepted a mission call to reclaim the "Brighamites" in Utah, on October 11, 1866, Emma wrote to Joseph III.

> As for Alexanders doing much with the Smiths at Salt Lake is a doub[t]ful question with me. I think it right for him to go and discharge his duty to them and leave them without excuse I look upon their case as a hard one I believe God is able to do all that is for his glory and the good of those that truly serve him, and may be that God may consider them in their ignorance and convict and convert them and cleanse them from their abominations and make them fit for more decent Society. I hope he will.[4]

On August 1, 1868 (1869) Emma again wrote to Joseph III,

> I tried before they [her sons Alexander and David] left here to give them an idea of what they might expect of Brigham and all of his ites but I suppose the impression was hardly sufficient to guard <their> feelings from such unexpected falsehoods and impious profanity as Brigham is capable of. I hope they will be able to bear with patience all the abuse they will have to meet. I do not like to have my children's feelings abused but I do like that Brigham show to all both saint and sinner that there is not the least particle of friendship existing between him and myself.[5]

---

2   Letter of Emma Smith Bidamon to Joseph Smith III, February 2, 1866 [sic, 1867], Emma Smith Papers, P4, f36, Church of Christ Archives, in Romig, *Emma's Family*, p. 77.

3   Letter of Emma Smith Bidamon to Joseph Smith III, August 19, 1866, Emma Smith Papers, P4, f31, Church of Christ Archives, in Romig, *Emma's Family*, pp. 62–63.

4   Letter of Emma Smith Bidamon to Joseph Smith III, October 11, 1866, Emma Smith Papers, P4, f32, Community of Christ Archives, in Romig, *Emma's Family*, pp. 65–66.

5   Letter of Emma Smith Bidamon to Joseph Smith III, August 1, 1868-69. Emma Smith Papers, P4, f40, Community of Christ Archives, in Romig, *Emma's Family*, p. 83. Spelling standardized.

Visitors from Utah

Emma was never a recluse. Managing a hotel kept her in the public eye. More than one hotel guest was from Utah, none more well-known in Church circles than her nephews Joseph F. Smith and Samuel H. B. Smith. When they arrived at the Mansion House, their cousin Frederick greeted them and took them to the room where Emma was working. "Mother, do you know these young men?" Frederick asked. Joseph F. Smith wrote, "She appeared to have forgotten Samuel but *me* She said she would have known anywhere because I looked so much like father!"6

Utah visitors Parley P. Pratt Jr. and Nels Madsen questioned Emma about Joseph Smith being a prophet of God:

> Pratt: Do you believe that your husband, Joseph Smith died true to his profession?
> Emma: I believe he was everything he professed to be.7

When a discussion ensued, Emma said, "You may think I was not a very good Saint not to go West, but I had a home here and did not go because I did not know what I should have there."8

Some Utah visitors had more to say about Lewis Bidamon than Emma. Joseph C. Rich wrote to Edward Hunter on Christmas Day in 1869: "[Emma] is the wife of a man who, even among his friends is reproached as a drunkard and an adulterer. Only recently an illegitimate child has been sent him, that calls Emma grandmother."9 Junius F. Wells also wrote of Lewis Bidamon: "He is a full robust, idle, tricky, dirty, specimen of the *homo genus*, who on short acquaintance was familiarly impudent. No one would think of taking offence from his conduct, he is so manifestly a plebian of the lower sort."10

A Difference of Opinion

It is a well-known fact that Emma and Brigham Young had differences of opinion on several topics. Historical documents do not hint of unresolved issues surfacing in Kirtland, Missouri, or Quincy. In fact, before Brigham departed on

---

6   Linda King Newell, "Cousins in Conflict: Joseph Smith III and Joseph F. Smith," The John Whitmer Historical Association 9 (1989): 3–16.
7   Madsen, "Visit to Mrs. Emma Smith Bidamon [sic] 1931," as cited in Newell and Avery, *Mormon Enigma*, pp. 297.
8   Madsen, "Visit to Mrs. Emma Smith Bidamon [sic] 1931," as cited in Newell and Avery, *Mormon Enigma*, p. 298.
9   *Deseret Evening News,* January 7, 1870.
10 Journal of Junius F. Wells, April 21, 1876, as cited in Joni Wilson, "Emma's Enduring Compassion: A Person Reflection," *Nauvoo Journal*, 69. mormonhistoricsites.org.

a mission to the British Isles, he and his wife, Mary Ann, named their daughter Roxy Emma Alice Young and called her "Emma."

In an attempt to trace where the unresolved issues began, historical evidence suggests that it may have started with the printing of a hymnbook. On October 27, 1839, five weeks after Brigham left for England, the Nauvoo High Council "*Voted*, that Sister Emma Smith select and publish a hymn-book for the use of the Church, and that Brigham Young be informed of this action and he not publish the Hymns taken by him from Commerce."[11] Brigham did not receive word of the high council vote. "We are printing 3,000 copies of a hymn book," he wrote to his wife, Mary Ann, in June 1840.[12] When Brigham wrote to Mary Ann in November 1840, he informed her of receiving a letter from Joseph Smith: "In Brother Joseph's letter he sent to the twelve he said he had somethings against them, according to what I could learn from the letter it was because we did not wright to him upon the subject of printing the hymnbook."[13]

A second disagreement between Emma and Brigham Young followed the martyrdom of Joseph Smith. The issue was property—Joseph had not written a will and had not distinguished between personal and Church property. Then there was the question of ownership of Joseph's translation of the Bible. A small issue regarding a military parade in Nauvoo added fuel to an already unsettling relationship. For the parade, Brigham Young attired himself in the same uniform worn by Joseph Smith. From Joseph's ornate sword to his favorite horse, Jo Duncan, Brigham looked like his slain predecessor. As he reviewed the soldiers in the Nauvoo Legion, General J. J. Hardin and staff looked on. What was the issue? Twelve-year-old Joseph III fitted out the horse for the occasion with a "saddle, housings, holsters, and bridle. After the parade, Brigham's clerk rode the horse to exhaustion, which infuriated young Joseph, who resolved never to put a saddle on a horse for Brigham Young again."[14]

Then, of course, there was the decision of Emma not to follow Brigham Young to the Rockies. Emma suspected her decision was the reason she was being watched. Her son Joseph III wrote of her suspicions:

> Sometime in the Summer of 1845, or possibly in the Fall, mother was made aware that she was an object of suspicion to the leading element of the Church; and that a watch was set

---

11   Smith, *History of the Church*, 4:17–18.
12   Letter of Brigham Young to Mary Ann Young, June 1840, as cited in Newell and Avery, *Mormon Enigma*, p. 88. Spelling standardized.
13   Ibid.
14   Valeen Tippetts Avery and Linda King Newel, "The Lion and the Lady: Brigham Young and Emma Smith," *Utah Historical Quarterly* 48, no. 1 (Winter 1980): 93–94.

over herself and her household. Persons visiting her house were watched and their footsteps dogged; some were turned away from her door, without being permitted to hold communication with the household; and upon one occasion a man, a friend, was assaulted, and but for his resolute defense of himself, would have suffered severely. . . .

A trusted member of the church . . . waited upon mother to ascertain what her feelings were in reference to following the church west. She informed him that she thought she would not go . . . The elder . . . finally stated to her that it had been decided to offer her an opportunity to go; and that if she refused, it was "decided to make her so poor that she would be glad to beg pardon of the Twelve and follow them."[15]

The issue that most often surfaces in discussions of disagreements between Emma and Brigham Young was her stance against the doctrine of plural marriage and her adamant denial that Joseph Smith taught or practiced the doctrine. Although Emma succeeded in convincing her children that Joseph never taught or practiced the doctrine, she did not convince Brigham Young or members of the Quorum of the Twelve. Church leadership made disparaging remarks against Emma for her unwavering position on plural marriage. On July 12, 1857, Heber C. Kimball said, "What!—sustain a woman, a wife, in preference to sustaining the Prophet Joseph, brother Brigham, and his brethren! Your religion is vain when you take that course. . . . That was the trouble with Emma Smith. Joseph stood for the truth and maintained it; she stuck against it, and where is she? She is where she is, and she will not escape until Joseph Smith opens the door and lets her out."[16]

In April 1867, Jason T. Briggs, a member of the Reorganized Church of Jesus Christ of Latter Day Saints, reported an interview he had with Emma. During the interview, Briggs asked Emma about polygamy.

> J. W. Briggs—Mrs. Bidamon, have you seen the revelation on polygamy, published by Orson Pratt, in the *Seer*, in 1852?
> Mrs. B.—I have.
> J. W. B.—Have you read it?
> Mrs. B.—I have read it, and heard it read.

---

15 "Biography of Joseph Smith III," in Romig, *Emma's Family*, p. 57.
16 Heber C. Kimball, "The Latter-Day Kingdom—Men not to Be Governed By Their Wives—Love to God Manifested By Love to His Servants," *Journal of Discourses* 5: 28–29.

> J. W. B.—Did you ever see that document in manuscript, previous to its publication, by Pratt?
> Mrs. B.—I never did.
> J. W. B.—Did you ever see any document of that kind, purporting to be a revelation, to authorize polygamy?
> Mrs. B.—No; I never did.
> J. W. B.—Did Joseph Smith ever teach you the principles of polygamy, as being revealed to him, or as a correct and righteous principle?
> Mrs. B.—He never did.
> J. W. B.—What about that statement of Brigham Young, that you burnt the original manuscript of that revelation?
> Mrs. B.—It is false in all its parts, *made out of the whole cloth*, without any foundation in truth.[17]

In 1879 Emma's sons, Alexander and Joseph III, also asked Emma about polygamy:

> Q. What about the revelation on Polygamy? Did Joseph Smith have anything like it? What of spiritual wifery?
> A. There was no revelation on either polygamy, or spiritual wives. There were some rumors of something of the sort, of which I asked my husband. He assured me that all there was of it was, that, in a chat about plural wives, he had said, "Well, such a system might possibly be, if everybody was agreed to it, and would behave as they should; but they would not; and, besides, it was contrary to the will of heaven."
>
> No such thing as polygamy, or spiritual wifery, was taught, publically or privately, before my husband's death, that I have now, or ever had any knowledge of.
> Q. Did he not have other wives than yourself?
> A. He had no other wife but me; nor did he to my knowledge ever have.
> Q. Did he not hold marital relation with women other than yourself?
> A. He did not have improper relations with any woman that ever came to my knowledge.
> Q. Was there nothing about spiritual wives that you recollect?

---

17 *The History of the Reorganized Church of Jesus Christ of Latter Day Saints*, 5 vols. (Independence, MO.: Herald House, 1967), 3:352.

A. At one time my husband came to me and asked me if I had heard certain rumors about spiritual marriages, or anything of the kind; and assured me that if I had, that they were without foundation; that there was no such doctrine, and never should be with his knowledge, or consent. I know that he had no other wife or wives than myself, in any sense, either spiritual or otherwise.[18]

Her granddaughter Emma Smith McCallum spoke of Emma's abhorrence of polygamy—

[Grandmother] abhorred polyg[amy] —can
see her yet as she'd
stand up & denounce
the charge of polyg[amy].
She was of iron will
truthfulness —If Jos[eph]
had had anyth[ing] to do
with polyg[amy] —she
would not [have stood] by him
or all the years [she] testif[ied]
to a lie
She was hated
because of this stand[19]

On May 14, 1882, Elder Wilford Woodruff said at a Sunday meeting in the Tabernacle in Salt Lake City,

Emma Smith, the widow of the Prophet, is said to have maintained to her dying moments that her husband had nothing to do with the patriarchal order of marriage, but that it was Brigham Young that got that up. I bear record before God, angels and men that Joseph Smith received that revelation; and I bear record that Emma Smith gave her husband in marriage [to] several women while he was living, some of whom are to-day living in this city, and some may be present in this congregation, and who, if called upon, would confirm my words.[20]

---

18 "Last Testimony of Sister Emma," *The Saints' Herald* 20, no. 19 (October 1, 1879): 1.
19 Notebook of Interviews. Emma Smith McCallum's Reminiscences, in Youngreen, *Reflections of Emma*, pp. 67–69.
20 Wilford Woodruff, "Liberty of Conscience," *Journal of Discourses*, 23:131.

But it was more than Emma's stance on plural marriage that troubled President Brigham Young and other Church leaders. Emma's support of her son Joseph III's claim to authority to lead his father's church was a direct challenge to the leadership of Brigham. On October 1, 1866, at the general conference in Salt Lake City, Brigham Young said, "To my certain knowledge Emma Smith is one of the damnedest liars I know of on this earth; yet there is no good thing I would refuse to do for her, if she would only be a righteous woman."[21]

Three years later, on October 7, 1869, in the Tabernacle, Orson Pratt said, "That same woman [Emma] . . . has instilled the bitterest principles of apostasy into their minds [her sons], to fight against the Church that has come to these mountains according to the predictions of Joseph."[22] On August 24, 1872, in Farmington, Utah, Brigham Young said:

> We would be very glad to have the privilege of saying that the children of Joseph Smith, Junior, the Prophet of God, were firm in the faith of the Gospel, and following in the footsteps of their father. But what are they doing? Trying to blot out every vestige of the work their father performed on the earth. Their mission is to endeavor to obliterate every particle of his doctrine, his faith, and doings. These boys are not following Joseph Smith, but Emma Bidamon. Every person who hearkens to what they say, hearkens to the will and wishes of Emma Bidamon. The boys, themselves, have no will, no mind, no judgement independent of their mother. I do not want to talk about them. I am sorry for them, and I have my own faith in regard to them. I think the Lord will find them by and by.[23]

Neither distance nor time solved the controversies that existed between Emma and Church leaders. Could direct communication have resolved some issues? Perhaps. At least there would be dialogue. This is one of the unfortunate chapters in our history.

---

21 Report of Brigham Young's address on October 6–8, 1866 at the semi-annual General Conference held in the Bowery in Salt Lake City, in Elden J. Watson, "Brigham Young Addresses, 1865–1869." February 1982, p. 2.
22 Orson Pratt, "Celestial Marriage," *Journal of Discourses,* 13:194.
23 Brigham Young, "Increase of Saints since Joseph Smith's death—Joseph Smith's sons—Resurrection and Millennial Work," *Journal of Discourses,* 15:136.

Chapter Ten

THE LAST YEARS

On January 19, 1841, Joseph Smith received a revelation instructing him to construct the Nauvoo House as "a delightful habitation for man, and a resting-place for the weary traveler, that he may contemplate the glory of Zion" (D&C 124:60). The Prophet Joseph donated the land on which the Nauvoo House was constructed. In return for his donation, he and his descendants were to receive rooms in the house for perpetual use.

Title of the Nauvoo House

The title of the Nauvoo House passed to his widow, Emma, in June 1844 after the martyrdom. Work on the house continued under her ownership. On August 18, 1845, John Taylor wrote in his journal, "This morning they commenced laying brick on the Nauvoo House. I was present when they commenced. Elder Kimball made a prayer on the occasion; there were a great number of bricklayers on hand ready to commence and all seemed to enjoy good spirits."[1] In 1845, work on the house ceased as emphasis turned to finishing the Nauvoo Temple.

The building remained an empty shell until Lewis Bidamon tore down the extremities of the L-shaped structure and used the brick to build a two-story house on the southwest corner of the original building. The new structure has been known as the Bidamon House and the Riverside Mansion. Lewis and Emma moved into the Riverside Mansion in 1871. The Riverside Mansion was Emma's residence for nearly eight years.

A Broken Arm

Emma broke her arm in 1872, one year after moving into the Riverside Mansion. Her granddaughter Emma Smith McCallum's cryptic note explains how Emma broke her arm—

---

1 Dean Jesse, "The John Taylor Nauvoo Journal: January 1845–September 1845," *BYU Studies* 23, no. 3 (Summer 1983): 84–85.

> Maj. B[idamon]. had two large
> vineyards. [He] made [a]lot of
> wine. [He] made stair steps
> to cellar wide [in the Mansion House] —to put
> barrels of wine. She took
> milk &c up & down to keep
> cool. She fell & broke
> [her] work arm—may not have been
> set right or had to
> use it too soon—crooked
> bent not twisted.[2]

The accident was reported in the *Deseret News* in August 1872: "Emma had her arm in a sling, having falling down the cellar quite recently and broken her left arm just above the wrist, which she said was doing well."[3]

Other than a broken arm, Emma's health remained good. As she aged, Emma often took a nap after a heavy noon meal, and when she read, she wore spectacles, much like other older women of her era. Emma tended to her flowers but was not often seen tending to her large garden. She continued to receive visitors, but not with as much frequency as in days gone by. Of those who visited, none were more important to Emma than her children and grandchildren who she loved very much. Other than an occasional outing, her life was centered in Nauvoo and in her family. She was happiest when surrounded by loved ones.

Death of Emma Smith Bidamon

As Emma's life began to ebb in the spring of 1879, for two weeks family members were at her bedside. Her son Joseph III kept a day-by-day journal of her last days in April 1879:

> Tuesday, April 22: Found Alex here at Nauvoo and Julia in care of mother. Mrs. Abercrombie doing the work of the house.
>
> Wednesday, April 23 . . . Mother apparently failing . . . Slight rain . . . Cherries in blossom. The old place looks lovely but oh! how desolate.
>
> Thursday, April 24 . . . Slept splendidly so still, so pleasant. Clouds over the sky this am . . . Mother continues to fail. Food fails to stimulate her.

---

2 Notebook of Interviews. Emma Smith McCallum's Reminiscences, in Youngreen, *Reflections of Emma*, pp. 68–59.

3 *Deseret News*, August 9, 1872.

> Friday, April 25 . . . Mother fails more rapidly. Has taken no nourishment for some hours, her pulse grows feeble constantly . . . her breath labored.
> Saturday, April 26 . . . Mother quite bad.
> Sunday, April 27. . . Was up with mother till 4:30. She was very bad. Did not think she would live till morning.[4]

On Tuesday, April 29 Emma's son Alexander wrote to his wife Lizzie:

> Mother is gradually failing, she cannot recognize anyone now. Her mind wanders constantly. Poor mother, Oh, Lizzie, it is hard to see her suffer so. We do all we can for her and still she suffers fearfully . . . We are simply waiting the end, and it seems to be near, only God knows how near. I think sometimes I have passed through the worst, yet I know how hard it will be to give mother up.[5]

In the evening hours of April 30, Emma's sons, Joseph III and Alexander, alternated turns sitting near her bedside. Alexander heard his mother call out, "Joseph, Joseph, Joseph." He awakened his brother, Joseph III, who hurried to his mother's bedside. Joseph saw his mother raise up and extend her left arm as she said, "Joseph! Yes, yes, I'm coming."

"Mother, what is it?" Alexander asked, but his mother did not reply, for she was dead.[6] Emma died at 4:20 a.m. at age seventy-four.

Eulogies of Emma Smith Bidamon

Emma's body was prepared for burial and covered in "a dress brocaded with leaves and magenta flowers."[7] Her remains were laid in a casket in the parlor of the Mansion House. As mourners passed through the parlor, they spoke in whispered tones about the life of Emma.

Funeral services for Emma were held at 2:00 p.m. on May 2, 1879. J. A. Crawford, a minister in the Reorganized Church of Jesus Christ of Latter Day Saints, was the principal speaker. He based his funeral text on Job 14:14—"If a man die, shall he live again?" At the close of the service, J. H. Lake paid tribute to Emma's faith and hope. Her remains were then buried in the Smith cemetery in Nauvoo.

---

4   Joseph Smith III Journal, April 1879, as quoted in Newell and Avery, *Mormon Enigma*, p. 304.
5   Letter of Alexander Smith to Lizzie Smith, April 28–29, 1879, as quoted in Newell and Avery, *Mormon Enigma*, p. 304.
6   *Zion's Ensign*, December 31, 1903, as cited in Newell and Avery, *Mormon Enigma*, p. 304.
7   Newell and Avery, *Mormon Enigma*, p. 305.

On July 15, 1879, the Reorganization held a memorial service in honor of Emma in Plano, Illinois. On that occasion, Mark H. Forscutt of the Reorganization gave a two-hour eulogy praising her. Her son Joseph Smith III in the *Saints' Herald* of May 15, 1879, also praised his mother:

> My mother was one of the best poised women I ever met. Of the purest and noblest intentions herself, she never submitted to be made a party to anything low, wrong, or evil, was absolutely fearless where the right was concerned; and was a just and generous mother. Her heart never changed toward her children, and her fidelity to them never wavered. It's needless to say that we *loved* her.
> —Joseph Smith III[8]

An announcement of Emma's passing appeared in "A Poem to Alexander H. Smith upon the Passing of His Mother" by J. A. Crawford. One stanza reads:

> God be praised, thy aged mother
> Did not pass behind the veil;
> 'Till she heard the proclamation,
> Ushering in the restoration.[9]

On May 21, 1879, an announcement of Emma's death appeared in the *Deseret News*: "To old members of this Church the deceased was well known, as a lady of more than ordinary intelligence and force of character."[10] The *Woman's Exponent* of May 15, 1879, printed,

> Mrs. Emma Bidamon, died in Nauvoo on the 30th of April. Among the Latter-day Saints, in days gone by, she was familiarly known as "Sister Emma," wife of the Prophet Joseph Smith. She was considered rather a remarkable woman, possessing great influence and unusually strong characteristics, which if properly directed, as in the early days of this Church, would have made her name illustrious in the history of the women of the Latter-day Saints down to the end of time.[11]

---

8   Joseph Smith III, "Editorial Items," *Saints' Herald* 26, no. 10 (May 15, 1879): 152.
9   Joseph A. Crawford, "To Brother Alexander H. Smith," *Saints' Herald* 26, no. 15 (June 15, 1879): 180.
10 "Death of Emma Smith," *Deseret News* 28, no. 16 (May 21, 1879): 243.
11 "Home Affairs," *Woman's Exponent* 7, no. 24 (May 15, 1879): 243, as cited in Newell and Avery, *Mormon Enigma*, p. 305.

On September 9, 1940, Charles Edward Bidamon, the son of Lewis Bidamon and Nancy Abercrombie, wrote a tribute to Emma:

> I was taken into the home of Emma Smith Bidamon in 1868, at the age of four years, and was considered as one of the family up to and including the year of her death in 1879.
>
> As to my recollection of her, she was a person of a very even temper. I never heard her say an unkind word, or raise her voice in anger or contention.
>
> She was loved and respected by the entire community, (all who knew her). And at her funeral, which the whole countryside attended, many tears flowed, showing grief at her passing. She had a queenly bearing without the arrogance of a queen. A noble woman, showing and living a charity for all. Loving and beloved . . .
>
> Her children and grandchildren visited her oft-times and loved and esteemed her highly. But I was there continually from the age of four in 1868 until her death in 1879, a period of eleven years. I should know her disposition and character thoroughly. Her ideals were high and her disposition kindly.[12]

As to Emma's burial site, as the years passed, questions arose as to where Emma, Joseph, and Hyrum Smith were buried. In 1928, W. O. Hands was appointed to direct a small group of surveyors and engineers to search for their graves. They began digging on January 9, 1928, and found the graves seven days later on January 16. The remains of Joseph, Hyrum, and Emma were exhumed and placed in silk-lined wooden boxes. The boxes were placed side by side. The bodies were reburied on Friday, January 20, 1928, and the graves marked.

In 1991, under the joint direction of leaders of the Reorganized Church of Jesus Christ of Latter Day Saints and leaders of The Church of Jesus Christ of Latter-day Saints, new tombstones were placed in a gardenlike cemetery near the Homestead in Nauvoo. On August 4, 1991, the renovated cemetery was dedicated by Wallace B. Smith, great-grandson of Joseph Smith and president of the Reorganized Church of Jesus Christ of Latter Day Saints. At the ceremony, Elder M. Russell Ballard, a great-great-grandson of Hyrum Smith, represented The Church of Jesus Christ of Latter-day Saints.

---

12   Charles E. Bidamon to Warren L. Van Dine, September 9, 1940, as cited in Youngreen, *Reflections of Emma*, 84–85, fn. 44. See also Charles E. Bidamon to L. L. Hudson, August 10, 1940, Church History Library.

Celebrating the Life of Emma Smith

Emma Hale Smith is arguably the most famous LDS woman of the nineteenth century, yet she did not leave a journal, autobiography, and but few letters. Gratefully, contemporaries wrote of her life—none more so than her husband Joseph Smith.

To the Prophet Joseph, she was "My beloved Emma, she that was my wife, even the wife of my youth; and the choice of my heart . . . undaunted, firm and unwavering, unchangeable, affectionate Emma!"[13] His journal entries tell of his attentive care of her: "Emma began to be sick with fever; consequently I kept in the house with her all day. . . Emma is no better. I was with her all day."[14] His letters reveal his abiding love for Emma: "I would gladly go from here to you barefoot and bareheaded, and half naked, to see you and think it great pleasure."[15] It is not surprising that Joseph pled on behalf of Emma and their children: "Have mercy, O Lord, upon [my] wife and children, that they may be exalted in thy presence, and preserved by thy fostering hand" (Doctrine and Covenants 109:69).

Emma was the first to know that Joseph Smith received the gold plates from the angel Moroni, and they were kept under the bed in her small home in Harmony, Pennsylvania. They "often lay on the table without any attempt at concealment, wrapped in a small linen table cloth, which I had given him to fold them in. I once felt of the plates, as they thus lay on the table, tracing their outline and shape." To Emma, the plates "seemed to be pliable like thick paper, and would rustle with a metallic sound when the edges were moved by the thumb, as one does sometimes thumb the edges of a book."[16]

She was the only woman to serve as a scribe for the Book of Mormon translation. Joseph wrote, "I have again commenced translating, and Emma writes for me." Emma recalled that as Joseph was translating he "could not pronounce the word *Sarah*." He asked, "'Emma, did Jerusalem have walls surround it?' When I informed him that it had, said Emma, Joseph replied, 'Oh! I was afraid I had been deceived.'"[17]

Of her role as scribe, Emma said,

> My belief is that the Book of Mormon is of divine authenticity—I have not the slightest doubt of it. I am satisfied that

---

13 Journal, December 1841–December 1842, p. 164, Joseph Smith Papers.
14 Smith, *History of the Church*, 5:166–167.
15 Letter of Joseph Smith to Emma Smith, April 4, 1839. Joseph Smith Papers.
16 "Last Testimony of Sister Emma," *Saints' Herald* 26, no. 19 (October 1, 1879): 290.
17 Emma Smith to Edmund C. Briggs, "A Visit to Nauvoo in 1856," *Journal of History* 9 (January 1916): 454.

> no man could have dictated the writing of the manuscript unless he was inspired; for, when acting as his scribe, your father [this was said to Joseph Smith III] would dictate to me hour after hour; and when returning after meals, or after interruptions, he could at once begin where he had left off, without either seeing the manuscript or having any portion of it read to him. This was a usual thing for him to do. It would have been improbable that a learned man could do this; and, for one so ignorant and unlearned as he was it was simply impossible.[18]

Her testimony of the Book of Mormon and the prophetic calling of her husband led to her baptism on June 28, 1830, by Oliver Cowdery. Less than a month after she entered baptismal waters, Joseph Smith received an important revelation for Emma in which she was told, "Behold, thy sins are forgiven thee, and thou art an elect lady, whom I have called" (D&Cs 25:3). The revelation was personal for Emma, yet Latter-day prophets have used it as counsel for all women.

She compiled a pocket-sized hymnbook titled *A Collection of Sacred Hymns for the Church of the Latter Day Saints*, which contained ninety hymns. The songs of praise in the small book speak volumes of her love for the Lord and the Restoration of the gospel.

Emma became the mother of eleven children, raising five to adulthood. With two babies in her arms and two children at her skirts, Emma walked across the frozen Mississippi River, carrying Joseph Smith's papers, including the new translation of the Bible. "No one but God, knows the reflections of my mind and the feelings of my heart when I left our house and home, almost all of everything that we possessed excepting our little Children," Emma wrote to Joseph, "and took my journey out of the State of Missouri, leaving you shut up in that lonesome prison [in Liberty]."[19]

Emma graciously welcomed both the poor and the acclaimed into her home and was the president of the Female Relief Society of Nauvoo. Under her guidance, women searched out those in need and ministered to them. Through their service, heavy burdens were lifted, sorrows too severe to be carried alone were shared, and necessities required to sustain life were freely proffered.

Emma participated in temple ordinance work, acting as proxy for extended family members. She wrote letters in defense of Joseph Smith to the governor of

---

18 "Last Testimony of Sister Emma," *Saints' Herald* 26, no. 19 (October 1, 1879): 290.
19 Letter of Emma Smith to Joseph Smith, March 1839. Joseph Smith Papers.

Illinois, even traveling to Quincy to meet with him on this important matter. She cared for Lucy Mack Smith for five years as Lucy suffered from crippling arthritis. Mother Smith said of Emma, "I have never seen a woman in my life, who would endure every species of fatigue and hardship, from month to month, and from year to year, with that unflinching courage, zeal and patience, which she has always done."[20]

Emma maintained and preserved properties in Nauvoo that were of significance to the life of Joseph Smith and the Latter-day Saints. In her seventy-fourth year, in speaking of Joseph's prophetic calling, she said she believed "he was everything he professed to be."[21]

Due to kind remembrances of loved ones, especially Joseph Smith, there is much known and much to celebrate about the life of Emma Smith, including the promise in her patriarchal blessing: "Thou shalt be saved in the kingdom of God; even so, Amen."[22]

---

20 Lucy Mack Smith, History, 1845, p. 190. Joseph Smith Papers.
21 "Last Testimony of Sister Emma," *Saints' Herald* 26, no. 19 (October 1, 1879), 290.
22 Patriarchal Blessing given to Emma Smith by Joseph Smith Sr., December 9, 1834. Kirtland, Ohio, in Marquardt, *Early Patriarchal Blessings*, p. 15.

Epilogue

THE FOLLOWING IS A BRIEF account of Emma Smith Bidamon's family:

Lewis Bidamon

Lewis Bidamon was age seventy-two at the death of Emma, his wife of thirty-two years. Following her death, Lewis resided with his son Charles "Charlie" Edward Bidamon in the Riverside Mansion in Nauvoo. On May 15, 1880, Lewis married Charlie's mother, Nancy Abercrombie.

In his final years, Lewis often asked visitors to read passages from the Bible and Book of Mormon to him. Joseph III asked his stepfather if he would like to be baptized. In response to the question, "[Lewis] looked me squarely in the face . . . with tears trickling over his whitened cheeks and said, "Joseph, *it is too late!*" Joseph asked, "Too late, Major?" He replied, "Yes, my boy; it is too late. . . . Lord be merciful to me, a sinner."[1]

Lewis is remembered for leading the Fourth of July parades in Nauvoo until senility and old age left him practically helpless. His wife Nancy cared for him until his death on February 11, 1891. In his last will and testament, Lewis left his widow, Nancy, "the East half of the . . . Riverside Mansion . . . One half of the garret . . . equal privileges of the halls and stairs below and above . . . one half of the cellar . . . and full ingress and egress to and from the privy on the premises."[2] After the death of Lewis Bidamon, Nancy moved to Kansas City, Missouri, where she died on July 30, 1903.

Julia Murdock Smith

In 1848, seventeen-year-old Julia, adopted daughter of Emma and Joseph, became acquainted with Elisha Dixon, an unemployed "magician" boarding at

---

1   Joseph Smith III, *Memoirs of President Joseph Smith* . . . appearing in the *Saints' Herald* (November 6, 1934–July 31, 1937), as cited in Newell and Avery, *Mormon Enigma*, p. 306.
2   L. C. Bidamon, Last Will and Testament, in Wilson, *Emma's Enduring Compassion, A Personal Reflection*, p. 76.

the Mansion House. At the time, Elisha was age thirty-six and suffering from ill health. Apparently, Julia "took delight in taking the 'gypsy king' his meals and reading to him as he rested and recovered."[3] In the spring of 1848, Elisha and Julia eloped and were married in St. Louis.

In 1852, Julia and Elisha were living near Galveston Bay, Texas. Elisha worked on the steamboat *Magnolia* which took excursion trips on the Trinity River out of Galveston. On an excursion, Elisha was severely burned when the boiler on the steamboat exploded. He suffered for three weeks before his death. Following his demise, Julia packed her bags and returned to her mother in Nauvoo.

In Nauvoo city, twenty-two-year-old Julia captured the fancy of John Middleton. Although John was a devout Catholic, they were married on November 19, 1856, by Reverend Waldenmeyer, the minister of the Presbyterian Church in Nauvoo. A year after their marriage, on November 9, 1857, Julia joined her husband in the Catholic faith, being baptized at the Church of St. Francis Xavier in St. Louis.

John Middleton became an alcoholic. Julia ended her marital relationship with John and returned to Nauvoo in 1876. A few years later, her mother, Emma, died on Julia's birthday—Julia lost both of her mothers on April 30 (one in 1831 and the other in 1879). In 1880, Julia was diagnosed with breast cancer. She died on September 10, 1880. Her obituary appeared in the *Nauvoo Independent* newspaper:

> [Julia] was a woman of the most exemplary character—an advocate of all the graces and all the virtues and had a strong loving disposition for her friends which firmly endeared them to her. She was considerably about the medium of intelligence and of a[n] indomitable spirit which manifested itself in the trying ordeal of sickness through which she passed . . . She leaves many friends who deeply regret her death.[4]

Joseph Smith III

In January 1855, Joseph III moved to Canton, Illinois, to study law with the Honorable William Kellogg, an attorney in Fulton County. Joseph III wrote, "I remained there the better part of a year, visiting home in the spring and being present at the death of Grandmother Smith in May . . . I returned

---

3 Cecil McGavin, *The Family of Joseph Smith*, p. 179, as cited in Murdock, *Joseph and Emma's Julia*, p. 83.
4 *Nauvoo Independent*, September 10, 1880, as cited in Murdock, *Joseph and Emma's Julia*, p. 164.

home in 1856, owing to the want of means to continue my studies at Canton, and began farm life with my brother Frederick as my partner . . . October 22d of this year I was married to Miss Emaline Griswold."[5]

In April 1860 at a conference of the Reorganization in Amboy, Illinois, on a motion of Isaac Sheen, it was "resolved, that Brother Joseph Smith be chosen Prophet, Seer, and Revelator of the Church of Jesus Christ, and the successor of his father."[6] Joseph III was ordained president of the high priesthood by Zenos Gurley, Samuel Powers, William W. Blair, and William Marks.

Joseph III called his brothers Alexander and David Hyrum Smith as apostles in the Reorganization. David poetically penned of their role in the Reorganization:

> Joseph is the Chosen Prophet;
> Well ordained in God's clear sight,
> Should he loose by his transgression,
> Alexander has the right.
> Joseph, Alexander, David
> Three remaining pillars still
> Like the three remaining columns
> Of the Temple on the hill!
> Joseph's star is full and shining;
> . . . Mine is just below the mountain;
> Bide its time and it will shine.[7]

Joseph III was president of the Reorganized Church of Jesus Christ of Latter Day Saints for fifty-four years. On December 10, 1914, he died at his home in Independence, Missouri, at age eighty-two.

Frederick Granger Williams Smith

In 1856, Frederick and his brother Joseph III became partners in a farming enterprise. The enterprise was an economic failure. By the winter of 1858, the brothers were $2,500 in debt.

Frederick married Anna Maria Jones on September 13, 1857. To their union was born Anna Fredericka Smith. Frederick and his family resided on the Smith farm in Nauvoo. There Frederick suffered from a lingering illness assumed to be tuberculosis. By December 1861, his wife had abandoned him and taken their daughter with her.

---

5   "Biography of Joseph Smith III," in Romig, *Emma's Family*, p. 58.
6   *History of the Reorganized Church*, 3:250.
7   See F. Mark McKiernan, "David H. Smith: A Son of the Prophet," *BYU Studies Quarterly* 18, no. 2 (Winter 1978): 234–236.

Frederick moved into the Mansion House where he was cared for by his mother until his death on April 13, 1862, at age twenty-six. When the body of Frederick Smith was buried in the Smith cemetery near the Joseph Smith Homestead, church bells tolled twenty-six times for each year of his life.

David Hyrum Smith penned a "Memorial to Frederick G. W. Smith":

> He has suffered long and borne it well,
> His sorrows came thick and fast,
> Oh call him not back in pain to dwell,
> He has gone to sleep at last. . . .
>
> Then go dig him a grave on the warm hillside,
> 'Neath the shade of the green locust tree;
> Where the birds will sing; and the wild flowers bloom,
> And the long grasses wave mournfully.
>
> You know how he loved the sweet sunshine,
> And wished it might shine for aye,
> He has gone to the land where the father and son,
> Will make it forever day.
>
> Then weep, mother weep, and bow thy head,
> O'er the corpse so still and white;
> Yes, give to thy grief a little sway,
> E're they bear him from thy sight.
>
> They gathered around with a mournful tread,
> The couch where a brother was laid;
> They have folded his hands and have combed his head,
> And have laid him away with the dead.
>
> They have filled his grave on the warm hillside,
> 'Neath the shade of the green locust tree;
> Where the birds have sung, and the wild flowers have sprung,
> And the long grasses waves mournfully.[8]

Alexander Hale Smith

Alexander never joined a religious sect until his brother Joseph III became president of the Reorganized Church of Jesus Christ of Latter Day Saints. In

---

8   David H. and Clara Smith Papers, n.d., P78-1, f3, Community of Christ Archives. In Romig, *Emma's Family*, p. 119.

1866, Alexander ventured across the plains to California with a span of small mules, a pony, and a wagon. His journey was fraught with perils, hardships, and dangers but was not his last journey to the west. Alexander was a preacher of the Reorganization from the Atlantic to the Pacific.

On his journey to the western states in 1866, Alexander wrote to his mother:

> I feel all alone many times, and long to return to my Mother, my Mate, and my little ones. And had not God said to me, as he did, to my Father before me, "Seek ye first to establish the Kingdom of God and his righteousness, and all things else shall be added unto you. For the Lord knoweth thou has need of these things" I should not now be a pilgrim, wandering far from home, and those I love. As I tramp up and down, from place to place I friend many who remember to have seen my Mother and they all, desire to be remembered to her in loving kindness.[9]

When not on an assignment preaching in the Great Lakes, Hawaii, Utah, or the southern states, Alexander made his home in Illinois. In the spring of 1876, he removed to Andover, Missouri, where he farmed for five years before joining his brother Joseph III in Independence, Missouri. In 1890, Alexander purchased a home in Lamoni, Iowa, where he resided the remainder of his life.

From 1873–1897, Alexander was an apostle of the Reorganized Church of Jesus Christ of Latter Day Saints. He later served as a counselor in the first presidency and president of the Order of Evangelists. On August 12, 1909, after a three-day illness, Alexander died in the Mansion House in Nauvoo. He was buried in the Rose Hill Cemetery in Lamoni, Iowa.

David Hyrum Smith

In his youth, David Hyrum Smith showed a propensity toward art. Artist Frederick Piercy wrote of nine-year-old David, "He is of a mild, studious disposition, and is passionately fond of drawing . . . seeming to be never so happy as when he has a pencil and paper in his hand."[10] In the 1860 census, David listed his profession as a "portrait painter."[11] Through the years, he was known as a painter, singer, and poet. He was often referred to as the "Sweet Singer of Israel."

---

9   Letter of Alexander H. Smith to Emma Bidamon, 1866 [1876]. MS 7464 f6, Church History Library, as cited in Romig, *Emma's Family*, p. 99.
10 James Linforth, ed., *Route from Liverpool to Great Salt Lake Valley* (Liverpool: Franklin D. Richards, 1885), p. 65.
11 US Federal Census, 1860.

In 1863 David was ordained an elder in the Reorganized Church of Jesus Christ of Latter Day Saints by Joseph Smith III and W. W. Blair. The ordination set in place his life's ambition for the next decade. He penned to his brother Joseph III:

> Amidst the mighty rush of war [Civil War]
> By which the nation's troubles are
> Dissention grim
> The Lord (I feel with inward pride)
> Has drew me over on his side,
> To fight for him.[12]

David married Clara Charlotte Hartshorn on May 15, 1870. David and Clara made their home in the Mansion House for a time. David supported his wife as a missionary in the Midwest, Utah, Idaho, and California. As such, he was often away from home.

In Utah, it was rumored that David questioned his faith. Some claimed that his struggles with religion led to "brain fever." Others claimed he suffered a nervous breakdown. Unaware of David's mental state or concerns about his faith, Joseph Smith III called him to be a counselor in the presidency of the Reorganized Church of Jesus Christ of Latter Day Saints. In David's absence, Joseph Smith III had him sustained as a member of the presidency. When David returned to the Midwest, it was obvious to family and friends that at age twenty-eight his mind was clouded by mental illness. His moods ranged from high to low as did his temperament. His mother cared for him and confided in a visitor that "David's imbecility was her greatest trouble."[13] As the days passed, this "Sweet Singer of Israel" became delusional.

On January 19, 1877, at age thirty-two, David was committed to the Northern Illinois Hospital and Asylum for the Insane at Elgin, Illinois. Initially, family members thought that he would recover. Due to such thinking, David was not immediately released from his position in the presidency of the Reorganization. After twenty-seven years of confinement in the asylum, David died in 1904 at age fifty-nine.

---

12 David Hyrum Smith poem to "Dear Brother" December 22, 1861, Nauvoo, IL, as quoted in Avery, *From Mission to Madness,* p. 57.
13 Junius F. Wells Diary, March 14, 1876, as quoted in Avery, *From Mission to Madness,* p. 225.

Chronology

OF EMMA HALE SMITH BIDAMON

July 10, 1804	Emma Hale, daughter of Isaac Hale and Elizabeth Lewis, is born in Harmony, Susquehanna County, Pennsylvania.
1802–1825	Emma grows to maturity in Harmony.
October 1825	Emma meets Joseph Smith.
January 18, 1827	Joseph and Emma are married in South Bainbridge, New York.
September 22, 1827	Emma is the first to learn that Joseph has the golden plates.
June 25, 1828	Emma gives birth to Alvin Smith in Harmony; baby Alvin dies.
June 28, 1830	Emma is baptized a member of the Church of Christ by Oliver Cowdery.
July 1830	Emma is the subject of a revelation to Joseph (D&C 25).
February 1, 1831	Joseph and Emma arrive in Kirtland, Ohio.
April 30, 1831	Emma gives birth to twins in Kirtland; the twins die.
May 1831	Emma becomes the adoptive mother of twins—Joseph and Julia Murdock.
September 11, 1831	Joseph, Emma, and the Murdock twins begin residing in Hiram, Ohio.
March 29, 1832	Joseph Murdock dies from complications of measles at age 11 months.

May 1, 1832	W. W. Phelps is "ordered by the Council that the Hymns selected by sister Emma be corrected."[1]
June 6, 1832	Joseph writes to Emma from Greenville, Indiana: "I am happy to find that you are still in the faith of Christ."[2]
October 13, 1832	Joseph writes to Emma from New York City: "Thoughts of home of Emma and Julia rushes upon my mind like a flood."[3]
November 6, 1832	Emma gives birth to Joseph Smith III in an upper room of the Gilbert and Whitney store.
March 6, 1833	Joseph writes to Emma about the need to "commit the cross plow unto the hands of the poor."[4]
May 19, 1834	Joseph writes to Emma from Richmond, Indiana: "I pray God to let his blessings to rest upon you and the children."[5]
June 4, 1834	Joseph writes to Emma from the banks of the Mississippi River: "We all enjoy the fruits of our labour if we hold out faithful to the end which I pray may be the happy lot of us all."[6]
December 9, 1834	Joseph Smith Sr. gives Emma a patriarchal blessing; Oliver Cowdery is the scribe.
September 14, 1835	Emma is assigned "to make a selection of sacred hymns, . . . and W. W. Phelps be appointed to revise and arrange them for printing."[7]
1836	*A Collection of Sacred Hymns for the Church of the Latter Day Saints* is published.
March 27, 1836	Joseph petitions the Lord, "Have mercy, O Lord, upon [my] wife and children, that they may be exalted in thy presence, and preserved by thy fostering hand" (D&C 109:69).

---

1   Minutes, 30 April 1832, p. 26. Joseph Smith Papers.
2   Letter to Emma Smith, 6 June 1832, p. 3.
3   Letter of Joseph Smith to Emma Smith, 13 October 1832, p. [2], Joseph Smith Papers. Spelling standardized.
4   Letter of Joseph Smith to Emma Smith, March 6, 1833. Joseph Smith Papers.
5   Letter of Joseph Smith to Emma Smith, 18 May 1834, p. [1], Joseph Smith Papers. Spelling standardized.
6   Letter to Emma Smith, 4 June 1834, p. 58.
7   Minutes, 14 September 1835, p. 108.

June 20, 1836	Emma gives birth to Frederick Granger Williams Smith in Kirtland.
August 19, 1836	Joseph writes to Emma from Salem, Massachusetts: "You may know that you and the children are much on my mind."[8]
January 12, 1838	Joseph leaves Kirtland to escape mob violence; Emma travels to Far West, Missouri.
June 2, 1838	Emma gives birth to Alexander Hale Smith in Far West.
November 4, 1838	Joseph writes to Emma from Independence, Missouri: "I would inform you that I am well, and that we are all of us in good spirits as regards our own fate."[9]
November 12, 1838	Joseph writes to Emma from Richmond, Missouri: "I received your letter which I read over and over again, it was a sweet morsel to me."[10]
December 1, 1838	Joseph writes to Emma from Liberty, Missouri: "We arrived in Liberty and [were] committed to jail this evening but we are all in good spirits."[11]
December 1838	Emma visits Joseph in Liberty Jail.
February 15, 1839	Emma and her children leave Missouri by crossing the Mississippi River to reach Quincy, Illinois.
March 7, 1839	Emma writes to Joseph from Quincy: "No one but God, knows the reflections of my mind and the feelings of my heart when I left our house and home, and almost all of everything that we possessed excepting our little children, and took my journey out of the State of Missouri."[12]

---

8   Letter to Emma Smith, 19 August 1836.
9   Joseph Smith to Emma Smith, November 4, 1838, Church History Library. Spelling standardized; Letter to Emma Smith, 4 November 1838, pgs. 1–3. Joseph Smith Papers.
10 Letter of Joseph Smith to Emma Smith, 12 November 1838, pgs. 1–2, Joseph Smith Papers. Spelling standardized.
11 Letter of Joseph Smith to Emma Smith, 1 December 1838, p. [1], Joseph Smith Papers. Spelling standardized.
12 Letter of Emma Smith to Joseph Smith, 7 March 1839, p. 37, Joseph Smith Papers. Spelling standardized.

March 21, 1839	Joseph writes to Emma from Liberty Jail: "I want to be with you very much but the powers of mobocracy is too many at present."[13]
April 4, 1839	Joseph writes to Emma from Liberty Jail: "I would gladly go from here to you barefoot, and bareheaded, and half naked, to see you and think it great pleasure."[14]
April 22, 1839	Joseph joins Emma in Quincy after escaping from his captors in Missouri.
May 10, 1839	Joseph, Emma, and their children move to Commerce, Illinois.
October 27, 1839	The High Council of Nauvoo votes that "Sister Emma Smith select and publish a hymn-book for the use of the church."[15]
November 9, 1839	Joseph writes to Emma from Springfield, Illinois: "Believe me [my] feelings are of the best kind towards you."[16]
January 20, 1840	Joseph writes to Emma from Philadelphia: "The time seems long that I am deprived of your society."[17]
June 13, 1840	Emma gives birth to Don Carlos Smith in Nauvoo.
November 1, 1840	The *Times and Seasons* announces that Emma will compile another hymnal.
1841	Emma compiles a hymnal, consisting of 304 hymns.
1842	Emma gives birth to an unnamed son in Nauvoo.
March 17, 1842	Emma is elected president of the Female Relief Society of Nauvoo.
August 16, 1842	Joseph writes to Emma while in hiding: "Tongue cannot express the gratitude of my heart, for the warm and true-hearted friendship you have manifested."[18]

---

13 Letter to Emma Smith, 21 March 1839.
14 Letter of Joseph Smith to Emma Smith, April 4, 1839.
15 "History of Joseph Smith," *Latter-day Saints' Millennial Star* 17 (1855): 372.
16 Letter to Emma Smith, 9 November 1839, p. 1.
17 Letter of Joseph Smith to Emma, January 20, 1840, as cited in Dean C. Jessee, *The Personal Writings of Joseph Smith*, (Salt Lake City: Deseret Book, 1984), p. 454
18 Letter of Joseph Smith to Emma Smith, 16 August 1842, pgs. 173–75. Joseph Smith Papers.

August 17, 1842	Emma writes to Governor Thomas Carlin of Illinois: "May I entreat your Excellency to lighten the hand of oppression and persecution which is laid upon me and my family."[19]
August 27, 1842	Emma writes to Governor Thomas Carlin: "I entreat your honor . . . [to stop] persecution that you are well aware, is entirely without any just—foundation or excuse."[20]
July 1, 1843	Joseph records a revelation on the new and everlasting covenant of marriage (D&C 132); Emma rejects the revelation.
August 31, 1843	Joseph, Emma, and their children move into the Mansion House in Nauvoo.
June 23, 1844	Joseph writes to Emma from Iowa: "May God Almighty bless you & the children & Mother & all my friends."[21]
June 25, 1844	Joseph writes to Emma from Carthage, Illinois: "Myself & Hyrum have been again arrested—for Treason."[22]
June 27, 1844	Joseph writes to Emma: "I am very much resigned to my lot knowing I am justified and have done the best that could be done give my love to the children and all my friends."[23] A mob kills Joseph and his brother Hyrum in Carthage.
November 17, 1844	Emma gives birth to David Hyrum Smith in Nauvoo.
December 9, 1845	The *New York Sun* prints a November 20, 1845, letter signed by Emma Smith; Emma renounces the letter as a forgery; her denial is printed in the *Times and Seasons* on January 15, 1846.
September 11, 1846	Fire damages the Mansion House during the Battle of Nauvoo.

---

19 Journal, December 1841–December 1842, p. 177, Joseph Smith Papers.
20 History, 1838-1856, volume D-1 [1 August 1842-1 July 1843], p. 1387, Joseph Smith Papers.
21 Letter to Emma Smith, 23 June 1844, p. 1, Joseph Smith Papers.
22 Letter of Joseph Smith to Emma Smith, June 25, 1844, History, 1838–1856, volume F-1 [1 May 1844–8 August 1844], p. 157, Joseph Smith Papers.
23 Letter of Joseph Smith to Emma Smith, 27 June 1844, pgs. 1–[2], Joseph Smith Papers. Spelling standardized.

September 12, 1846	Emma and her children take passage on the steamer *Uncle Toby* to Fulton, Illinois; in Fulton, Emma rents a house.
February 1847	Emma and her children return to Nauvoo; Emma opens the Mansion House as a hotel.
December 23, 1847	Emma marries Lewis Crum Bidamon; Reverend William Haney, a Methodist minister, performs the service.
1849	Lewis Bidamon journeys to the goldfields of California; Emma remains in Nauvoo.
January 7, 1850	Emma writes to Lewis Bidamon from Nauvoo: "I have scarcely enjoyed any good thing since you left home."[24]
April 6, 1860	Emma is welcomed as a member of the Reorganized Church of Jesus Christ of Latter Day Saints (RLDS).
June 28, 1860	Emma is visited by her nephew Joseph F. Smith; Joseph F. recalls, "[Emma] said she would have known me anywhere because I looked so much like father!"[25]
1861	Emma compiles *Latter Day Saints' Selection of Hymns* for the RLDS Church.
1871	Emma moves from the Mansion House to a brick house, known as the Riverside Mansion, near the Mississippi River in Nauvoo.
1872	Emma falls down the cellar steps in the Mansion House and fractures her left arm.
February 4–10, 1879	Emma is interviewed by her son Joseph Smith III; the interview is printed in the *Saints' Herald* on October 1, 1879.
April 30, 1879	Emma dies in Nauvoo at age seventy-four.
May 2, 1879	Emma is buried next to Joseph Smith Jr. in the Smith family graveyard in Nauvoo.

---

24 Letter of Emma Smith Bidamon to Lewis C. Bidamon, January 7, 1850, pp. 26–30, as cited in Romig, *Emma's Family*, pp. 26–30. Spelling standardized.

25 Linda King Newell, "Cousins in Conflict: Joseph Smith III and Joseph F. Smith," *The John Whitmer Historical Association* 9 (1989): 3–16.

About the Author

DR. SUSAN EASTON BLACK JOINED the faculty of Brigham Young University in 1978 and taught Church history and doctrine until she retired to serve multiple missions with her husband, George Durrant. She is also past associate dean of general education and honors and director of Church history in the Religious Studies Center.

The recipient of numerous academic awards, she received the Karl G. Maeser Distinguished Faculty Lecturer Award in 2000, the highest award given a professor on the BYU Provo campus. Susan has authored, edited, and compiled more than 100 books and more than 250 articles.